T0193230

'FURRINERS'
in Appalachia

'FURRINERS'
in
Appalachia

MARJORIE U. CONDER

'FURRINERS' IN APPALACHIA

iUniverse books may be ordered through booksellers or by contacting:

iUniverse
1663 Liberty Drive
Bloomington, IN 47403
www.iuniverse.com
1-800-Authors (1-800-288-4677)

ISBN: 978-1-5320-8408-9 (sc)
ISBN: 978-1-5320-9536-8 (e)

Library of Congress Control Number: 2020902982

Print information available on the last page.

iUniverse rev. date: 03/19/2020

For Steve, who shared the journey with me,
and
For Ruth, who helped make this book possible.

CONTENTS

ACKNOWLEDGEMENTS

Deepest thanks to those who helped make my story a better one. Douglas Starr, PhD, Professor Emeritus of Communications, Texas A&M University, corrected mistakes in the manuscript; Chris Day, Editor for iUniverse, helped put the story into a better format; writer and friend Michelle Morrison encouraged from afar with insightful comments; writer friend Pam Keating made helpful suggestions; my Munds Park writing group critiqued the very rough draft; Vy Armour gave me publishing tips; and many other friends helped along the way with encouragement and love. I owe them all for their help.

This book would not have happened without those people who encouraged me to write it. My husband, Steve Conder, urged me to write our memories of the incredible four years we spent in the hills of Kentucky. His recollections of incidents and descriptions of Kentucky coal mining were invaluable. To all my family and to the many friends who kept pushing me to finish the story after his death, thank you.

AUTHOR'S NOTE

Due to the passage of many years since my story took place,
some of the names of people and places mentioned
in this book may not be accurate.
Any errors are mine.

CHAPTER 1

Welcome to Kentucky

It was seeing the guns that got to me.

When my husband first drove our baby son and me into the small Kentucky mountain town on a sultry June afternoon in 1951, the empty street surprised me. The quiet seemed unnatural. The only sounds were the hum of the engine and the swish of our tires on the pavement. In spite of the oppressive heat, the strange silence gave me goose pimples.

I didn't like the look of this little town of Hyden at all.

"Where are all the people?" I asked Steve, uneasily.

"I don't know," Steve said. "I can't imagine where everyone is. It's really strange to see the street so empty, though this *is* Sunday."

He had no more commented on the lack of people when we spotted a small group of men—maybe five or six—standing on the corner.

"Oh, look! There are some people," I said, poking Steve's arm. "Maybe it's only the awful heat keeping everyone inside." The heat and humidity made for a muggy atmosphere; it was not a good day to be outside.

However, my relief lasted only a few seconds. As we drove closer,

I saw that the men, most of them dressed in denim overalls over bare chests or white T-shirts, cradled rifles and shotguns in their arms or wore pistols on their hips. No wonder no one else was around.

That's when I panicked.

I had not expected to see guns carried openly on the main street of town. Even though I had grown up in the West, I'd never seen men carrying guns in town, except for policemen. The people I knew in my hometown in Arizona who had guns used rifles and shotguns to go deer or quail hunting. And most of the ranchers we knew carried guns when they rode out on the range. But guns on a street corner? In town?

I clutched the baby tightly as if I could protect his little body from gunfire. Tired and fretful after the long drive from Knoxville and the longer flight from Arizona, he began to cry. I patted his back to soothe him, but I wished that somebody would soothe me.

"Steve, look! Do you see all those guns?" I asked, my voice trembling. I punched Steve's arm again, harder this time. "What is going on here?"

"I do see the guns, and I'm not really sure what's going on. I've not seen them on the streets before." Steve had just started working for a nearby coal mining company and had been staying in a Hyden boarding house for the past month. He paused.

"Hmm. Maybe the local nonunion miners are expecting union organizers from Harlan County. Those organizers have been trying to stir up trouble here, trying to pressure the nonunion miners to join the union."

His words didn't help. All I could see were the guns. Maybe we were in for a gunfight between the miners and the organizers? *Dear God, keep them from shooting.*

"Can't we go another way to get around them?"

"Nope. Only one street."

"Well, *hurry* then. We need to g-g-get past them."

The men glowered as we passed by the corner where they had gathered. I knew that our out-of-state license plate marked us as strangers, and I could feel a blanket of hostility wrapping around us. *Oh, God. Will they think we're organizers? Will they shoot at us?*

"We've got to get out of here *now!*" I whispered to Steve, as if the men could hear me.

"Take it easy, honey," he said, trying to reassure me. "We'll be past them in just a sec."

I was not reassured. Perspiration ran down my face—and not just from the heat. I gritted my teeth and shut my eyes, expecting to hear a gunshot at any minute. It didn't help that the baby, feeling my agitation, began to whimper again.

Steve sped up, heading for the boardinghouse. From the time we entered Hyden, the few minutes it took to get through the town seemed like an eternity.

"Well, here's the boardinghouse," Steve said, pulling up to the building where we would live until our apartment in the coal camp was ready for us.

"Thank God we're here." I felt a great weariness, as if I'd undergone some huge cataclysmic event. Even though we were safe, I would not forget those moments when I thought our lives were in danger.

Until that Sunday, Steve had no reason to worry about violence in Hyden. He had just started his first job after college as an engineer for a coal mining company that had both union and nonunion mines, so he was aware of the explosive tensions between the organizers and the nonunion miners. However, he had not noticed any real threat until that afternoon when we saw the local miners geared up for the possibility of a gun battle.

This was not what I expected when I learned that we were moving to Kentucky. I thought that moving to this southern state sounded like a lovely adventure. The South always evoked a romantic mystery for me, colored by *Gone with the Wind* and other tales of the southern writers I'd studied in school. When Steve started his job in the mountains of eastern Kentucky that summer of 1951, I didn't really expect white-pillared mansions, but the guns thoroughly shattered my romantic image.

What I hadn't envisioned was the brutal reality of poverty, ignorance, and violence at that time in Appalachia, the name given later to the hills of Kentucky, Tennessee, and West Virginia.

Here, I learned, every man had guns, and they often settled disputes with their guns.

Nothing in my life had prepared me for this. From that first day until we left Kentucky four years later, the common use of guns in violent acts created a deep-seated fear that was always lurking somewhere in the back of my mind.

We had ventured into a veritable foreign country, complete with unexpected violence, a new language to learn, unfamiliar customs, and strangers who viewed us with suspicion as foreigners, or as they said, *furriners*.

I had much to learn.

CHAPTER 2

The Boardinghouse

When Steve stopped in front of the boardinghouse, I breathed a sigh of relief that the guns were behind us. I picked up the baby and hugged him tight. We were safe, at least for the time being. God had heard my silent prayer.

I took a minute to look up at the old building that would be our home for the next month or so. It was not much to look at from the outside, but I was glad to have any refuge from the scene down the street. The dilapidated two-story frame building looked like a sanctuary, peeling paint and all.

The plump, friendly landlady greeted us at the door. "Hi, Mistah Steve, and you must be Miss Margie," she said. "I'm Missus Combs. Y'all come on in, and git settled raht in. Y'all look tuckered out."

"We *are* tuckered out," I said, savoring the word *tuckered*. Though not a word I would have used, it seemed to fit my weariness. The interminable flight from Arizona to Knoxville with the baby on my lap, the long, hot drive from Knoxville to Hyden, and then the unfriendly

5

welcome had me completely undone. The cranky baby squirmed in my arms. We were tuckered out.

"I'm still shaking from seeing those men with guns down the street," I told her.

"Don't you worry none about them," she said. "They'll be gone in the mornin'. They's jist a-guardin' aginst union organizers."

So, Steve was right, but that didn't soothe me much. I needed some time to settle down.

However, I was happy to meet Mrs. Combs, whose friendly manner was a sharp contrast to the suspicious miners in the streets behind us. Her warm welcome made me feel better, enough so that the English teacher in me picked up on her soft southern words. I would learn that this was the lovely, lazy speech of the area, one that was very easy to pick up myself.

"And let me see that darlin' baby," the landlady went on. "Ain't he the cutest thing! What's his name?"

I couldn't help but smile. "His name is Toddy. He's eleven months old."

She held out her arms to him, and Toddy went willingly to her, sensing that she was someone he could trust.

"Give me some sugah, darlin'," she said in that lovely drawl as she gave him a big kiss on the cheek.

He smiled and stopped his fretting.

Sugar? I guessed that must mean a kiss, but it was a usage I'd not heard before. I would hear that sweet phrase, so common in the South, many more times in the coming months. It seemed very appropriate for the action.

I warmed up to Mrs. Combs right away. Anyone who admired my child was surely someone worth knowing. Her soft Kentucky twang, casual grammar, and unfamiliar vocabulary sounded charming. Besides, her warm, matter-of-fact manner began to ease my fears and made me feel more comfortable.

"Follow me," she said, still carrying Toddy.

She led us upstairs, and Steve followed us with my suitcases.

"This hyar is your room," she said, showing us into a large, inviting

6

bedroom. The sun pouring in through the western windows gave it a cheerful feel even though it added to the heat. Everything looked clean and neat, with a double bed, a dresser, and a crib for Toddy. A colorful handmade quilt served as the bedspread, and sheer curtains crisscrossed the windows.

"What a nice room," I said. "And such a beautiful quilt. I'm sure we'll be comfortable here." I began to relax a bit.

"We put a rockin' chair in here for you and the baby." Mrs. Combs pointed to a wooden chair with a cushion in the seat.

"Oh, it's perfect, Mrs. Combs. I'll use it to put the baby to sleep."

She handed Toddy back to me, and we followed her downstairs.

"The bathrooms are down hyar, and you'll take yer meals down hyar too," she said as she led the way down to the basement.

The old boardinghouse had been remodeled at some point in order to bring in plumbing for the kitchen and bathrooms. I realized that with our room on the second floor and the bathrooms in the basement every trip to the bathroom would require two long flights of stairs down and two long flights back up, all while lugging a heavy baby on one hip. Not a happy thought.

Suddenly, I began to fall apart. The guns, the heat, the hunger, the weariness, and a fretful baby hit me all at once. I lost it. My eyes filled with sudden, self-pitying tears. *What am I doing in this place? This old building is just the final straw.*

I shut my eyes and fought back the tears, struggling to regain my composure. I didn't want to let my dismay show to Steve or Mrs. Combs, walking ahead of me. After all, Steve had already been living here for a month, and he had managed to survive. I guessed I could too. I took several deep breaths, fighting for control.

Okay, it was old and inconvenient, I rationalized, with several flights of stairs to the small, dingy bathrooms. The lights might have been fifteen watts, not enough to see if your face was clean. I supposed I could handle all that. Our room was nice, and so was the landlady. Surely, I could deal with it for the week or two they said it would take to ready our apartment. I had no idea that we'd live there for closer to six weeks.

Mrs. Combs was winding up the tour. "This hyar is the dinin' room, and supper will be ready purty soon. Jist come on downstairs about five."

Hmm, *supper*, not *dinner*. Maybe she served a light meal on Sunday night. I was starved. Little did I know that I was in for a huge surprise that would be a happy end to a stressful day.

CHAPTER 3

Reflecting

Back in our room, I soothed my cranky baby in the rocking chair and put him down for a nap in the crib. Then I curled up on the bed for a much-needed rest myself while Steve picked up the newspaper I'd brought with me.

As I lay there, not yet recovered enough from the disturbing sight of those guns to sleep, the movie of the whole previous month replayed in my mind.

After his graduation from Colorado School of Mines, Steve had gone ahead from Denver to Kentucky, towing a U-Haul with our few possessions. He needed to get started in his new job as soon as possible, for we had no money to speak of after living on his G.I. Bill benefits for the past two years. Before he left, I had flown home to Arizona, skipping my graduation ceremony from the University of Denver. I spent time with my family so they could dote on their first grandchild and pamper me a bit after that last hectic year, finishing my student teaching, caring for a new baby and my husband, and commuting from Golden to Denver every school day.

Steve had picked up the baby and me at the Knoxville airport after the long flight from Arizona. I was so happy to see him after a long month's separation, and I couldn't get enough of him. Until this past month, we had not been separated in the two years since we married.

"I missed you so much," I said, trying to hug him tightly with my one free arm, the other still holding Toddy.

"I missed you too," he said, wrapping his arms around both Toddy and me and planting a fierce kiss on my mouth. Oh, how I loved that man.

"I'm so glad to be here and together again, Steve."

"Me too." I saw the twinkle in his blue eyes as he grinned that devilish grin of his. Never much for mushy, emotional conversation, he just smiled and smiled as he looked at us. 'Nuf said.

"Let's get your luggage so we can get on the road."

I had eagerly looked forward to seeing our new Kentucky home. I couldn't wait to learn about a different part of the country, make new friends, and start our life together after four years of college.

I lay there remembering the first lovely impressions I had of the Appalachian Mountains earlier that day. The long, slow drive from Knoxville to Hyden on a narrow, winding two-lane highway allowed me to feast my eyes on the lush landscape. I marveled at the thick vegetation and magnificent forests of hardwood and pine trees.

The narrow Kentucky mountain road winds among
beautiful scenery, with trees on either side.

"Look, Steve, how beautiful the forests are! They're so thick you can't see around the next corner."

"They are pretty, but they make for slow driving."

Hmm, I thought. *Leave it to a man to see that and not the beauty.*

"They're nothing like the impressive Colorado forests, but they just have another kind of quiet beauty."

"Um-huh," he mumbled, intent on the winding road and oncoming traffic.

The richness of the land presented a stark contrast to the barren beauty of the high desert country where I had grown up along the Arizona-Mexico border. It seemed that God had painted everything green here: the trees, the shrubbery, the sunlight that filtered through the overhanging growth, and even the pavement, which reflected a pale-green hue. It *looked* cool and refreshing in spite of the heat.

As we climbed up higher into the mountains of eastern Tennessee and then into Kentucky, I was surprised to see that these ancient highlands looked like no more than steep hills covered with thick forests. Though small in comparison to the awesome, snow-covered peaks of the Colorado Rockies, I found these mountains possessed their own soft beauty of gentle curves, like rumpled pillows topped with splendid stands of trees.

Reflecting on that beautiful drive improved my disposition, and I felt far more cheerful after a lukewarm bath for Toddy and me in the tiny bathroom had cooled us off somewhat. Though I was still apprehensive about the guns, I felt even better after Steve gave me a detailed explanation of the union situation and the reason for the weapons.

"I told you that the unions have been picketing nonunion mines in Leslie County," he said. "The problem is that the nonunion mining companies naturally resist the union organizers because of the additional cost of their demands. Though most nonunion mines pay the same wages as union mines, other benefits demanded by the unions just cost too much, and the nonunion miners know there would be fewer jobs available if their bosses had to pay the costs of a union mine.

"These mountain men who work in nonunion mines are mostly

happy with their jobs that bring them fat paychecks," Steve explained further. "They are earning far more money than any of them ever saw until World War II started, about ten years ago, when they opened up the coal mines in this area. Before the war, most of these miners were really poor, working at hardscrabble farming or lumbering up in the hills and hollows. Now the average miner earns about twenty-five dollars per day—as much per shift as the union men."

"That's pretty good money, isn't it?"

"It is."

And it was in 1951.

"But the United Mine Workers have a long history of violence, encouraging their members to fight for better wages and benefits. For the unions, adding more miners to their rolls is what they really want; so, they keep trying to recruit the nonunion miners, sometimes by force, which can lead to bloodshed."

I finally got it. "I guess those men we saw today would resent outsiders coming in to tell them what to do, especially if they bring guns with them?"

"Right. So, there isn't any reason for you to be afraid. If any violence comes our way, it will be at the mine site. So, you needn't worry."

Not to worry—even though Steve will be at the mine site most of the time? I thought. I'm a good worrier. Confrontation between union and nonunion miners seemed very possible.

Although I now understood that the local miners were patrolling the streets only to keep the union men out, I still remembered the fear in my belly when I saw the guns so openly displayed as if the men were ready to pull the triggers. Somewhat mollified by Steve's explanation, I decided that there seemed to be little personal danger to us at that time, though I never forgot the fear. I still worried. As I said, I am a good worrier.

CHAPTER 4

Sunday Supper

What completely won me over that first day in Kentucky was not Steve's explanation about the miners and their guns so much as the memorable Sunday supper, my first meal in the boardinghouse.

Enticing cooking smells greeted us as we descended the stairs, and my mouth began to water with anticipation. I was starving.

"Mmm," I murmured to Steve. "Smell that?"

"Yup, can't wait."

"Is the food good here?"

"I've never gone hungry." Steve laughed.

"Are you hungry, Toddy?"

He gurgled happily, waving his arms.

The meal was a family affair, the first of hundreds of delicious southern repasts that we were to enjoy during our Kentucky sojourn. Three or four other boarders (all miners), the landlady and our little family sat around the one large dining table, filling the room to capacity. There was barely room for a highchair for Toddy.

"Y'all come on in and set yerselves down," said our landlady. So, we did, after tucking Toddy into the highchair.

Mrs. Combs did all the cooking with help from a young girl in the kitchen, and she served everything family style. Large bowls and platters of delicious delights filled the table and were passed around for everyone to help themselves. I was amazed. It was certainly not the light Sunday supper I had imagined. I would learn that supper in this part of Kentucky was the main meal of the day. And dinner, not lunch, was eaten at noon.

The table held a large platter of crisp-fried chicken; mounds of creamy mashed potatoes and at least a quart of gravy; endless ears of corn on the cob; a large platter of sliced, fire-engine red tomatoes; a bowl of fresh green beans; a cucumber and onion salad; turnip greens with vinegar to pour over; homemade bread-and-butter pickles; homemade biscuits with butter and homemade jam; and pitchers of sweetened iced tea. Fresh peach pie a la mode for dessert would add the final luscious few bites.

"Wow," I said. "Steve, look at all that food."

"It looks great, doesn't it?"

We sat down and filled our plates to overflowing.

"Pass the biscuits, please," said Steve. He does love biscuits and gravy.

"Mrs. Combs," I said. "This is all delicious. How do you make this wonderful cucumber salad?"

"Why, I jist soak them cucumbers and onion slices in vinegah and a little bit of sugah."

"That sounds simple to make. I'll have to try it."

"Shore 'nuf, it's real easy."

"Pass the gravy, please," said Steve. He was on his second biscuit. I don't know where he was putting it all. Eating was serious business for all the men there, and they didn't talk much during the meal. The array and the quantity were mind-boggling, and everything was delectable— even the dishes unfamiliar to my western palate, such as the turnip greens and the cucumber salad, even the sweetened iced tea. Steve was raised in Memphis, and he seemed familiar with all those southern dishes—and he was obviously delighted with the bounty on that table.

When we finished gorging ourselves, we staggered back up the stairs in a stupor, laid Toddy in his crib, and collapsed into bed. As I curled myself around Steve's back, I thought how great it was to eat so well and not even have to cook or do the dishes. At that point, I could barely remember my fears about the guns. Pushing them aside, I told myself, *everything is going to be all right*, and I drifted off to sleep.

Little did I know then that gun violence would continue to touch our lives during our four years in Kentucky.

CHAPTER 5

Furriner

The next morning, bright and early, Steve went off to the coal mine, carrying his lunch pail, which Mrs. Combs had packed for him. Sleepily, I waved goodbye and turned over in bed. Exhausted from the long trip and stress of the day before, I catnapped for a while, enjoying the luxury of sleeping in.

A wail from the crib finally awakened me. After a diaper change and a bottle, Toddy became his usual happy self, and we went downstairs for breakfast, smelling the delicious aroma of bacon cooking. There we found another lovely meal.

"Good morning, Mrs. Combs. What a lovely spread you have fixed!" I looked at all the serving bowls, many of them empty now.

"I'se got to feed them hungry miners a good breakfast so they can work all day," she explained.

A dish of fluffy scrambled eggs, plates of bacon and sausage, and flaky biscuits with butter and homemade jam (though she had gravy for the biscuits, too) presented a glowing testament to Mrs. Combs's expert culinary skills. I relished each bite, enjoying again the fact that I hadn't had to cook it and that someone else would wash the dishes.

Our genial landlady was bustling around the dining room, cleaning up dishes and food, and cooing at Toddy. "What a darlin' boy you are," she told him.

He gave her a jam-sticky grin as if he believed it too.

"Mrs. Combs, this breakfast is so good. Look, Toddy likes it too." He was smearing the scrambled eggs and jam all over his face with his chubby little hands.

"Yes, ma'am, he shore et good."

Thinking how good a walk to stretch my legs after breakfast would be, I asked, "Do you think those men and their guns are still out there today?"

"No, ma'am," she said. "They've done gone back to work."

"Do you think it's safe to walk around the town?"

"Shore 'nuf. You jist go have yerself a walk."

That was good news. I was curious to see what this little piece of Kentucky was like—as long as I could poke my head out the door without worrying about getting shot. Comfortably full, rested, and calmed down now from the frightening episode of the previous day, I cautiously peeked out the window.

Everything looked different in the morning light. The miners were gone from the corner, along with their guns. I could see a few women walking on their errands, some with small children. I still had some trepidation, but it did look safe, and I was eager to explore and get some exercise after sitting so long during the trip from Arizona the day before.

As soon as I cleaned up my sticky little boy, I asked him, "Want to go for a walk?" He clapped his hands happily as I put him in the stroller. We went out to see the town.

My first glance outside revealed the green, heavily wooded hillsides around Hyden's perimeter, wrapping the town like a protective embrace. The road disappeared into the woods in several directions. A few side streets crisscrossed the dusty main street, which ran several blocks long.

"Smell this wonderful air, Toddy," I said. I took a deep breath, enjoying the freshness. The cool of the morning felt wonderful compared to the previous afternoon's humid, enervating heat. As we walked toward the few stores, I felt excited all over again to discover what the people in my new home looked like.

"Look, Toddy, this is where we'll be living for a little while."

He kicked his legs furiously and waved his arms in answer. Obviously, I wasn't pushing the stroller fast enough.

Down the main street, I found storefronts containing typical small-town businesses: a food market sporting hand-printed flyers pasted on the windows; a drugstore where a scruffy brown dog lay panting near the door; a clothing store displaying a few simple dresses and hats in the window; a hardware store where pots and pans hung from the ceiling while saws and other tools covered the walls; and a dentist's office with windows too dusty to see through. I could see the county courthouse and a school nearby.

I saw a few women, some with children, walking down the street. The men must all be at work, I guessed. The women mostly wore mid-calf, print cotton housedresses, and their little girls wore similar dresses, down below their knees too. Most of the little boys sported faded denim overalls over bare chests or white T-shirts, like their daddies with the guns we'd seen the day before. Fascinated to see their clothing styles so different from home, I found it hard not to stare. The children stared back, but most of the women kept their eyes on the ground, not looking at me or Toddy. I found that a bit disconcerting, but I figured it was because they just didn't know me.

"Hello," I greeted several women, but most averted their eyes. No one seemed to *see* me. My tentative attempts at greeting people were met for the most part with an unintelligible mumble. I spoke to them politely, but only one responded with a quiet "Howdy." The western custom of speaking to people one meets on the street, if only a "Hi" or a "Hot day, isn't it?" is so common that I had no idea why no one responded to my overtures here in Hyden, Kentucky. Not only that, no one even stopped to admire Toddy in his stroller. Back home, a baby precipitated an instant introduction. I was a bit disappointed. *Is there something wrong with us?*

Observing how these mountain women were dressed, I began to

feel self-conscious about my summer sundress, with tiny shoulder straps and no sleeves. *Perhaps it is my dress that offends them? Is it too revealing? Maybe it's not appropriate in this part of Kentucky? Am I breaking the style rules here?*

I felt a bit embarrassed, but I needed to get some baby lotion, and the drugstore caught my attention. When I pushed the stroller around the dog and through the door, the lone clerk looked up. "Hep you?" she asked, a middle-aged woman who appeared old beyond her years. Her toothless gums caved in her mouth.

"Do you have any baby lotion?"

"Over thar." She pointed to the shelf.

I found the bottle and took it to the counter. "Do you know where I could find a newspaper?"

"Raht thar's the Hyden *Weekly*." She pointed me to the shelf.

"How much?"

"Twenty-five cents for the *Weekly*," she mumbled, "an' fitty cents for the lotion." She seemed lackadaisical in making the sale, but she happily took my money.

I tried to open a conversation. "Is it going to warm up again this afternoon?"

"Probly." She avoided looking at me, like the women in the street. *Darn, she's not very friendly either. What am I doing wrong?*

I gave up and went back to wander down the street, but I never succeeded in engaging anyone in conversation.

Discouraged, I decided to head back to the boardinghouse. "Well, that was not much fun," I told Toddy. "But don't you worry. We'll find some friends here." Clueless, but happy to hear me talking, he grinned back at me and babbled some unintelligible words. My heart responded with love for my precious child.

Walking back, I felt sad that my first foray into hill country society was unsuccessful in even carrying on a conversation with anyone but the drugstore clerk and my baby. "What am I doing here, Toddy? These people act as though I'm speaking a foreign language. Have I come to a foreign country?"

Unfortunately, he didn't have the answer.

I was to discover that this part of Kentucky *was* like a foreign country to me, one that I would have to learn about and adapt to their ways. I was truly a foreigner here. A *furriner*, as they said. Learning to live with these different ways and this different language would involve effort on my part. While I sometimes found that effort difficult, it was rewarding when I was successful.

Toddy just gabbled happily as I returned to my comfort zone of the boardinghouse. Mrs. Combs seemed to adore our baby and to like me too. *At least* she *accepted me*, I thought, a bit sadly. I was probably a furriner to Mrs. Combs too—even though it didn't seem to bother *her*.

Later, as I learned more about these good mountain people, I came to realize that maybe it was not just me but rather their natural reticence upon seeing a stranger from another part of the country in their small town that led to their reluctance to respond. They may not have been unfriendly so much as loath to speak to someone who obviously looked different, sounded different, and had come from strange parts. A furriner. But at the time, on my first full day in Kentucky, I was disheartened.

The gun-toting coal miners did not reappear on the streets of Hyden during the next week or two, and the threat of violence began to fade. Toddy and I walked every day, and I wore a skirt and a short-sleeved blouse. A day or so after my first walk, someone talked to me.

"That there's a cute baby," the man at the hardware store said. He was standing at the open door of his establishment. *I knew it! The baby is an icebreaker.*

"Uh, thanks," I answered, a bit startled to have someone notice us.

"How old is the little 'un?"

"One year in July." Surprised at his overture, I didn't know what else to say. I decided the weather might be a safe topic. "Think it will rain soon?" I asked. There were a few dark clouds on the horizon.

"Not yet," he said. "Too early. Mebbe later."

He turned and went inside, but I stood there for a moment, delighted to have had that brief conversation with someone. "See, Toddy? Maybe they are getting used to seeing me. I've broken the ice."

It felt good.

CHAPTER 6

Interlude

I so looked forward to Steve coming home from work that first day after we arrived. I was on pins and needles to fill my eyes with him again.

"I'm home," he announced as he came into our room.

I got up to give him a welcome-home hug, but then I stopped short. His blue eyes peered out from a black face. He was black all over—from head to toe.

"I guess you'll have to wait for that hug until you've cleaned up," I said, laughing at the sight of him.

"Yep, I'll go hit the bathtub as soon as I get these coveralls off."

He wore the coveralls over his khaki work clothes with the arms and legs taped tightly around his ankles and wrists and tucked into his work boots. The boots came off first, in a cloud of coal dust.

"Keep your distance," he warned.

The coveralls were filthy, and when he took them off, he sprayed more clouds of black dust all over the room. The khakis underneath were stained with another layer of the pervasive black grit. He looked like a refugee who had worn the same clothes for months. His hard hat had covered his head, protecting it somewhat, but when he took it off, I could see gray dust powdering his blond hair.

"Good grief," I said. "It looks like Mount Vesuvius erupted in here. Is it like this every day?"

"Every day," he said with a laugh.

"I should have known, since you were working in a coal mine."

Even after a bath, he still had black eyelashes and grime under his fingernails that he couldn't quite get out.

"I'm sore too," he said. "My back is killing me."

"What happened?"

"It's just that the seams of coal are only about three feet high, and the roof is just a bit higher. So, I have to duckwalk or crouch all day long. If I forget to crouch low enough for a second or if my leg muscles can't hold me in that position, I scrape my back on the roof of the mine."

We still have the hard hat he wore in the coal mines; the top is scratched and pitted from his constantly hitting it on the roof, a tangible reminder of what he went through those first hard weeks of work in the coal mines.

His back and thigh muscles ached for weeks until he strengthened them enough to adjust to crouching all day. He had sores and scabs and even boils on his back for months. As soon as we got one place healed up, he would scrape another to create a new sore.

It was hard, backbreaking work for all the miners, and particularly for novices like Steve. However, he loved his underground work, and I soon accepted that the hardships were worth it to him. So, I patched up his sores and kept my mouth shut. I knew that what was really important to him needed to be important to me too.

As the days went by, I started to relax and enjoy the novelty of living in a boardinghouse. I had no chores to speak of, no cooking, no dirty dishes, no cleaning, no shopping, just taking care of the baby and handwashing our personal clothing items. Steve's coal-blackened work clothes went to the laundry.

Our days settled into a routine: Waving goodbye to Steve as he went off to work. A bath after breakfast for Toddy and me. Washing our little laundry. A walk with a few tentative conversations. Lunch (more

24

good food). A nap for Toddy while I caught up with correspondence and reading. Then, a happy reunion with my coal-dusted husband. And finally, a sumptuous supper. We did enjoy those meals. I must have gained five or ten pounds during our stay in the boardinghouse.

Now that college was behind us, and Steve was gainfully employed, I couldn't help but indulge myself with a most welcome leisure time during that quiet interlude at the boardinghouse. It had been a frantic senior year for me at the University of Denver, which ended with graduation just a month earlier. Having a small baby, a full schedule of classes, student teaching, cooking, laundry, housecleaning, and a long commute for the past year, I had to organize every minute of my day. Now it was heaven to do just what I wanted when I wanted.

Steve's schedule at Colorado School of Mines had been a tough one too. His advanced engineering degree required as many as twenty-two or twenty-three credit hours of classes each semester—and twenty-six hours one brutal semester. We'd both been too busy to stop and smell the flowers.

Now we both had a new, different lifestyle. Steve had his job, which he loved. I, on the other hand, didn't know what to do with all my new leisure time. It felt good not to have to organize every minute of the day, but I also felt a bit at loose ends. I couldn't wait until we had our own place, and we could settle down to a normal life.

I wrote voluminous letters to friends and family during that period, reassuring myself that I had an identity with those I loved and those who loved me. I read everything I could get my hands on – magazines, books, and the few newspapers I could find. How wonderful to read for pleasure instead of studying dull textbooks.

Most especially, I played with Toddy. I loved having unlimited time to spend with our little boy, watching each stage of his development and enjoying his emerging personality. For most of his first year, while I was attending my college classes, he'd been looked after by a kindly woman who cared for him in her home during the day. Now I treasured the uninterrupted moments we shared. He was trying to walk, holding on to furniture, and babbling a few words. He could crawl faster than

I could easily catch him. He loved to build piles of his blocks and then knock them down, chortling with joy.

We would celebrate his first birthday in the middle of July. Such an adorable little guy; he amused me with everything he did, except when he woke us up in the middle of the night. Could there ever have been as wonderful a child as this? I know that every mother feels this way, but surely my child was unique and marvelous.

I was lonely, though, for adult companionship. I missed the stimulation of campus life and college classes and the comfort of understanding friends. Not knowing anyone except Mrs. Combs in Hyden, and not close enough to the coal camp and our apartment to get acquainted with my future neighbors, I really looked forward to Steve returning from work every afternoon. It was good to have adult conversation. We had so much to discuss: his new job, the men he worked with, Toddy's every new achievement, and the progress of our apartment construction, which wasn't coming along fast enough for me.

Would we *ever* get moved into our apartment?

CHAPTER 7

The Coal Camp

"Want to go for a ride to see the coal camp where the apartment is?" Steve asked me the next Saturday morning.

"Oh, yes! I can't wait. Just let me get Toddy ready."

Steve sweet-talked some sandwiches from Mrs. Combs, as I got our little son changed and dressed. I plunked him in his car seat—at that time, just a fabric seat attached to a metal frame that hung over the back of the front seat—and off we went.

The winding roads climbed up and down the steep mountains of Leslie County like a roller coaster. Between each one, a stream had cut a valley, a hollow, through the land, as if a knife had slashed a clearing between each hill.

"These hollows are called *hollers*," Steve said, "and the streams are *cricks*, not creeks. And the larger ones are *branches*."

"Ah, I'm learning some new language."

"And you'll learn even more too," he said. He was so right.

Most of the hollers were large enough to provide a couple of acres of arable land. Here and there, green cornstalks sprouted, along

Marjorie U. Conder

with tomatoes, beans, and other vegetables, in small plots near gray, unpainted cabins, many with tin roofs. Chickens scratched in dirt yards, where often we could see children at play. Some of the houses appeared run-down and uncared-for, a few surrounded by mounds of trash, old broken-down cars and rusty tools. An outhouse behind each home showed the lack of indoor plumbing, and we saw no electric lines. Poverty was obviously widespread, and living conditions were hard for these families.

Several rural Leslie County homes, built on a dirt path up the "holler." Mules and horses provided transportation for these residents in the 1950s as there were no roads for vehicles in many areas.

"Steve, everything looks so sad. How do these people make a living?"

"Most of them do a little farming, sell their crops and their calves or their pigs. They might do some lumbering or work odd jobs. Probably their best crop is their children; most families have lots of kids. They raise most of what they eat, but if they don't work in the coal mines, they live pretty hardscrabble lives. The men who live in these houses probably aren't miners.

"It's different for the miners," he explained. "If they go to work for the mines, they can earn a pretty good living. They have money in their pockets for the first time to provide better lives for their families. You'll see that almost all the miners' homes in the coal camp have a car parked in front. They can get to larger towns, such as Hazard or Harlan, to shop and see doctors."

In spite of those poignant sightings by the roadside, I enjoyed getting out on the weekend ride to see the lovely countryside where we would live for the next four years. Though these mountain people seemed poor in material possessions, they certainly were rich in the beauty and fertility of the land.

Not too many miles of winding roads east of Hyden led to the coal camp, several miles short of the little hamlet of Wooton. I couldn't contain my excitement as we drove down the hill to the coal camp that first time, wondering what our future home would look like.

"Here we are," said Steve as he pulled into the parking lot at the bottom of the hill. A large, gray cement block structure dominated the front of the coal camp. "This is the company store. They sell just about anything you need. The mine offices are in here, too."

The two-story building stocked groceries, hardware, chicken feed, tools, work clothes, and most everything else a family might want. Business seemed bustling, especially on a Saturday when the miners were not working, with cars and pickup trucks coming and going.

"Wow! This is great. Where is our apartment?" I asked.

"Look up," Steve said. "Our apartment is upstairs, there on the left, where you see the windows."

"I can't wait to see it!" I said, more anxious than ever to move in now that I could imagine what it might look like inside. "Do you think they might let us in to look?"

"I doubt it," Steve answered. "Probably no one is working today. It's Saturday."

"Okay." I was disappointed but resigned to waiting a bit longer. It had already been too long for me, and I wanted to get on with our lives.

As I looked around at the rest of the coal camp, I could see, at the left side of the store, four or five neat brick homes lining the graveled side street. Their backyards stopped at the bank of a pretty good-sized stream.

"That's Cutshin Creek," Steve said, pointing.

"It would be a river in Arizona, not a creek."

"Pronounce it crick," Steve corrected me.

"Okay, crick. I'm learning. Who lives in those brick houses?"

"The managers and superintendent. The boss's brother and his wife live in that house." He pointed to one of the neat homes.

Behind the store and down the dusty street on the right, a number of weathered, unpainted frame houses were nestled into the hillside. The back of the homes sat on the steep hill, and the front porches perched on stilts overlooking the street, providing storage underneath. Each home had a wooden outhouse behind it and up the hill.

"And who lives in those houses on the hill?"

"Those are for face bosses, foremen, and other senior workers."

"What about all the other coal miners? Where do they live?"

"Mostly in their homes up in the hills and hollers around here." *Hollers, cricks, branches,* I thought, vocabulary lesson for today.

The unpainted homes on the right side of the street with their outhouses behind them faced the manicured green lawns and flowerbeds abloom with summer blossoms of the brick homes on the left. It was a picture of contrasts, and not a very pretty one, I thought. The miners' homes were clean and neat, but they certainly suffered by comparison with the company officials' homes. I've always had a thing about fairness, and this looked anything but fair.

"Steve, why are those homes so different than the brick houses?" I asked.

"Well, they may not be as fancy as the others, but they are really a step up from their former homes up in the hills," he said, defending the coal company that owned the houses.

"Oh," I said, "but shouldn't foremen have better houses?"

"These *are* better houses than they had before," said Steve. "They have electricity and running water, which they didn't have up in the hills. Most of them have cars now."

I could see big cars, mostly Cadillacs, parked in front of the houses.

Steve continued, "Living in the coal camp is so much more convenient for them to get to work or to a store for groceries. And they pay very little rent. So, they seem happy with these places."

"If they have running water, why do they still have outhouses behind their homes?"

"None of the miners' homes have indoor plumbing," Steve said. "Company officials planned to install bathrooms when they were building the houses, but at that time these mountain people said they'd rather have their outhouses, which they were accustomed to, in order to keep the house clean. They weren't familiar with modern conveniences such as plumbing and water heaters and running water in their houses."

"But where do they get their water?" I asked.

"From the well that serves the whole coal camp. The company installed water lines with spigots by the back door, where it is handy. They don't have to draw it from a well. They also have electricity, which they didn't have in those cabins up in the hills, so they consider themselves lucky with their 'modern' living conditions and the cheap rent for company housing."

I thought about that. "I guess the ten years since World War II that brought roads and electricity to this part of Kentucky was not enough time for people to accept big changes in their living conditions?"

"Well, they did accept some big changes, using electricity for lights, for instance, instead of using candles and oil lamps. Having a reliable source of water from a pipe instead of drawing it from a well. Having a car that can take them places their mules could not. And even having the electricity for a radio that provides the country music they love. But bringing these hill people into the twentieth century was not easy. They were isolated for several hundred years and they have a lot to catch up with."

It still seemed unfair to me. Every time I looked at the contrast between the two sides of the street, I thought about it. Unfortunately, I knew I could not do anything about it.

I took it all in, the store, the brick homes, the whole little community. Thick, green forest swept up the hillsides behind the miners' homes on the hill and across the creek behind the managers' homes, cradling the small coal camp clearing below. Imagining how it would look from overhead, I could see the little settlement like a postage stamp pasted on the small flat bottom of the hollow, er, holler.

Homes of coal mine workers perch on the hillside of Smith Coal Camp. The side wall of the author's home is seen on the left.

I could hardly wait until we could move into our own home, meet our neighbors, and start our new lives. "When do you think our apartment will be ready?" I asked.

"The boss told me it would be a couple of weeks more."

"I hope it will be only a couple of weeks more. I'm beginning to think it will never get done."

"Don't worry, Margie. It will get done when it gets done."

"I know." I sighed. I was impatient, longing to leave Hyden and get into our own place.

We spent most weekends that month driving over the winding mountain roads and exploring the hills and hollers of Leslie County. I feasted my eyes on the magnificent forest scenery, with the high, emerald green walls of pine and hardwood trees that bookended the road on both sides, often blocking the view of what might be around the next curve.

"Look, Steve! Aren't these trees wonderful? It's like driving through a green tunnel. It's so different from Arizona."

"Um-huh," he answered, having seen the trees every day on his way to work. It was not a novelty to him. "It's different, all right!"

Even though he wasn't too impressed, I filled my soul with the beauty of the gorgeous thick forests, such a novelty compared to the sparse vegetation of my high-desert home. I had grown up where distances appear endless and the skies are vast. In the West, one can easily see for forty or fifty miles. Here we were lucky to see forty or fifty feet in front of us, but that only made me wonder what was around the next curve. I never got tired of those drives through the awesome Kentucky mountains.

CHAPTER 8

The Apartment

"Guess what?" Steve wore a happy grin when he came home from work that day.

"What?" I knew something was up.

"We can move into the apartment next weekend!"

"REALLY?" You probably could have heard my reaction clear over in Perry County.

"Really."

The coal company had remodeled a large storeroom over the company store into a spacious residence for us. Local unskilled laborers had framed in five rooms, run the electricity, installed the plumbing, painted each room, and sanded and varnished the bare floorboards.

Each week, we had gotten the progress report, and each week, it was not good.

"The carpenter didn't show."

"They couldn't get anyone to pick up the paint."

"The finish on the floors isn't dry yet."

One excuse after another. I don't think they had even started the work until Steve arrived in Kentucky some weeks before I did, even though they knew we were coming. But now it was finished. I couldn't wait to see our apartment and get settled.

We had stayed in the boardinghouse for about six weeks, expecting each week to hear that we could move in. Each week, we were disappointed. I had waited impatiently, reading, writing letters, playing with Toddy, marking time. We had celebrated Toddy's first birthday in mid-July. It wasn't until the end of July that the apartment was finally finished.

Happily, we started packing. We said goodbye to Mrs. Combs, parting from her with some sadness. Our landlady was the first person I'd gotten to know in this new country, and I would miss her cheerful and unflagging kindness, not to mention the delicious meals she cooked for us. "Give me some sugah, darlin'," were her last words to our small son. And he did.

Although I'd certainly enjoyed the leisure and the good food at the boardinghouse, I was eager to spread my wings into more than one room and have our own things around us again. A larger bathroom with a decent light would be very nice, too.

As we drove over the winding mountain road that Saturday morning, I was filled with happy anticipation.

"We're moving into our own home, and it seems like we're finally beginning our new life here in Kentucky," I said. Our college days were behind us, and the world awaited us in the tiny community where we would live for the next four years.

"It will be good to have our own place," he said. "But today, we've got to get all our belongings out of the empty house where I stored it."

As we came down the steep hill, the coal camp opened up below us, set in the holler on one side of Cutshin Creek. *Crick*, that is. *Gotta start using the local language.* The little settlement bustled with cars, huge coal trucks, and busy people on this Saturday morning.

"Look, Toddy!" I pointed to the buildings at the bottom of the hill. "That's where we are going to live."

He babbled happily in reply.

"It really will be great to move in," said Steve. "I'll be glad to be closer to the mine site and not have that long drive twice a day." Ten miles in Arizona or Colorado usually took ten minutes. Here, the winding mountain roads meant double that time or more.

"And just think, you won't have to get up so early in the morning," I said.

"Yup. An added benefit."

"But the best part for me will be living with our own furniture and belongings again. I've almost forgotten what we have."

"You'll remember as soon as you see it all," Steve said.

"I guess so. I do fondly remember the washing machine. I can hardly wait to do our laundry in it instead of by hand in the bathroom basin."

Steve chuckled.

"And Toddy will have more room to play too."

"Here we are," Steve said as he turned off the highway. Driving between the company store on the right and the brick homes lining the left side of the street, he pulled into a parking area behind the store. "We go up those steep stairs at the back of the store to get access to the apartment."

"Wow, that's a big climb, but I can't wait to see everything!"

I still remember the joy I felt that day as we climbed those stairs, hauling Toddy and our suitcases. It literally took my breath away, though I'm not sure if that was due to the anticipation or to the steep steps.

At the top of the stairs, we opened the door into a foyer for three apartments. The large one on the left was a mirror image of ours on the right. A smaller apartment directly in front of us was squeezed in between the two others. Our front door opened into a nice-sized entryway with a big window at the back of the building, overlooking most of the houses in the coal camp.

"We're home, Toddy," I said. "Let's explore."

We dropped the suitcases, put Toddy down to crawl, and started to investigate this place where we would live.

A very long, dark hall ran the depth of the building, from our entryway at the back of the store to the living room at the front. All the other rooms opened onto the right side of the hall. It was a strange layout, but it was the best they could do with the space available.

"There's the kitchen." Steve pointed to the first door. Opening from the foyer, the kitchen-dining room was a pleasant sunny room with windows at the back and side of the building. I looked in for a quick assessment to see the basics: sink, stove, refrigerator, and cabinets.

Three bedrooms came next, all in a row, with a bathroom in between the first two.

"Here's our room," I said as we poked our heads into the first bedroom, a large room with ample space for furniture.

Then came the good-sized bathroom—yes, it had a decent light—and the second bedroom.

"This bedroom is yours, Toddy. Come see." He had developed a fast crawl and caught up with us to see another large bedroom. Our small son could scatter all the toys he wanted to in this room.

The third bedroom was a duplicate of the other two. "We can use this as a storeroom," Steve said.

"What a great idea," I said. "We have boxes of books and things that can go in here until we get bookcases and other furniture."

Finally, at the far end, the hall ended with a doorway into the living room, which overlooked the road at the front of the store. From the large front window, we could see back up the hill from which we had just come. The road disappeared in the distance, soon hidden by thick woods. Hyden was behind us now.

"Look at the hill from this window, Steve. We can see where we came from."

"You're right. We've come a long way," he said. "I'm thinking of the journey we made from a college campus to the Smith Coal Camp. We have a whole new life and a new home." He gave me a long hug.

"And it's so good to be here now," I said, hugging him back.

I reveled in the ample space. After living in small basement apartments in Denver, a veterans' housing project apartment, and then six weeks in just one bedroom in the boardinghouse, it felt wonderful to expand into all these rooms, even though we had very little with which to fill them.

We felt very lucky to have the new apartment, so bright and cheerful. At the back, we had spectacular views of the entire holler with the miners' wooden houses perched on the hillsides and the forested hills beyond them. From the side windows, we could see Cutshin Creek meandering behind the brick homes across the way. The hillside swept up behind the creek into dense forest. My new world sat under our windows like a birthday present waiting to be opened.

"Look, Steve. What a view!"

"Doesn't look much like Colorado, does it?"

"No, but these mountains have a different kind of beauty. They are soft and friendly compared to the towering Rockies. And I love the creek running through the hollow. Or should I say, 'the crick runnin' through the holler.'" I giggled a bit at using the unfamiliar language of this new country.

"It *is* a pretty view," Steve agreed.

"It's wonderful!" I said.

"It is indeed." He hugged me tight again, knowing how I had longed to get settled.

Once we had investigated all the rooms, the first order of business was retrieving our bits of furniture and boxed belongings. Steve had stored everything in an empty house in the coal camp for the almost three months since we left Colorado. It was close enough to walk to.

"Which house has our things?" I asked.

"First one on the right," he said as we walked up to the unpainted house. "We're here."

CHAPTER 9

Rats

The rotten odor overwhelmed us when Steve opened the front door to the house where our things were stored.

"What is that awful smell?" I asked.

"I can't imagine, Margie," he mumbled as he led the way into the small house, carrying Toddy under one arm. "I'll check it out."

I could barely see in the dim light. When my eyes adjusted, though, I saw chaos. Instead of neatly stacked boxes, numerous cartons were torn open and dumped over, their contents spilling onto the dirty floor. Everything was black with coal dust, and it all smelled disgusting.

"Oh, Steve." I shuddered. "What a mess. Everything is filthy! Don't put the baby down on the floor."

"Uh-oh, this doesn't look good."

It wasn't just coal dust dirty. Animals had torn open the boxes, and everything was covered with animal droppings. No wonder it smelled. *Blasted animals.*

"Oh, no!" I kept finding more damage. "They chewed on our books! And look at this chair. It has teeth marks on the legs."

After examining the mess, Steve knew the culprits. "Looks like rats have been in here."

My stomach churned. "Rats? That's disgusting." I felt as though I was going to vomit at the thought of rats defiling our belongings. "I can't believe this!"

"It'll be okay, Margie." Steve took a moment to comfort me before he started looking through everything. The evidence confirmed his diagnosis. The rats had torn open the moving cartons, leaving their filthy traces behind. Some of the books, including my precious Bible, had the spines chewed away; others were ruined by the rat urine and would have to be thrown out. Some of the boxes of clothing were wet, too.

We had so few possessions at that point in our life that they were all precious to me. My chest was heavy with anger and dismay; I knew the meaning of the word *heartsick*. I wiped away the angry tears because I didn't want Steve to see me acting like a spoiled child whose toys had been smashed. I tried to pull myself together and act like an adult, and Steve never knew the depth of my feelings. It wasn't his fault, and I wasn't about to burden him.

He was ever his practical self, the efficient engineer. "What we need to do is throw out what's ruined and get everything else up to the apartment so we can clean it up."

"You're right, of course." My voice was shaky. "But how are we ever going to get it all up those stairs?"

"I'll check at the store," he said. "They'll know someone who can help. And I'll take Toddy so he doesn't get dirty."

Moving the filthy furniture and torn boxes from the empty house to the apartment required physical help. Those long, steep stairs made it difficult for one person to carry anything heavy or awkward up them.

"Meanwhile, you can start tossing out things," he said.

"Okay." I gulped, almost gagging. It was a nasty job, but I gritted my teeth as I went through what was hopelessly ruined. It had to be done. I tossed out a few boxes of soiled items and sorted everything, but our few pieces of furniture were mostly just dirty and blackened with coal dust. Most of what had been packed in the boxes—the clothing, dishes and pots and pans—could be salvaged and cleaned. It wasn't *all* bad, but it was bad enough.

It was my biggest challenge in Kentucky so far—and certainly not one I'd expected. I had idealized having our own things in our new home, and the damage to our few precious possessions had popped the balloon of my joy.

When Steve came back, he had good news. "Two teenaged boys live in the apartment across from ours. I checked to see if they'd like to make some money."

Happily, they did. They made light work of that which would be difficult for the two of us alone. Steve helped the boys, and I carried Toddy back up the stairs and cleaned up with supplies from the diaper bag.

"Well, Toddy, this is a revolting development. Those darn, stinking rats!" I probably used stronger language; I was just so furious. He grinned, not understanding what was going on. No sympathy at all, darn it.

Once everything was in the apartment, most of it in the kitchen where I could clean it, I could survey the damage.

"Well, I best get to work," I said with a sigh. I had managed to tackle the mess the rats had made without bawling like a baby, but I still felt violated.

"I'll help, Margie," Steve said sympathetically.

I could either sit down and cry—or I could get to work. So, I got to work. It wasn't easy, but together we had at it.

We cleaned Toddy's crib first so he could have his nap in it. Fortunately, the mattress was covered with plastic, which I could easily clean with soapy water, along with the wooden crib itself. Once we scrubbed the slats and railings, I could see that the damage to the crib was minimal. Our other belongings were harder.

Holding my nose against the stench of rat urine, I washed, scrubbed, disinfected, rinsed and polished every dish, every pot, every fork, knife, and spoon, every piece of wedding silver, and each of our few pieces of furniture. After we cleaned up our old wringer washing machine, Steve hooked it up so we could wash every piece of clothing, every sheet, and every towel and blanket we had stored. It took the rest of that day and most of the following day, but I finally felt our possessions were clean.

Even though I wept a few private tears over the loss of some of my cherished things, I knew that material possessions could be replaced. The important thing was that Steve and I still had each other, our precious baby son, and a new home of our own. After two years of marriage, while finishing college with very little money, we were starting on a new, wonderful life together. We had a roomy apartment and a paycheck coming in twice a month. Life was good, in spite of the damage and loss.

I got over it eventually, but I'll not ever forget the rats.

CHAPTER 10

Nesting

Once all our cleaned-up furniture was placed in the hall of the apartment, we could see that the few pieces we owned would barely fill a corner of each room. Fortunately, the company had furnished the kitchen with the essentials: stove, refrigerator, sink, and cabinets. Our old wringer washing machine fit nicely into a corner. The kitchen was separated from the eating area by a waist-high counter.

"I'll set up the card table if you'll take care of the chairs," I said. The small folding table was the only one we had. In Colorado, we had rented some essential furniture, including a table.

"Will do."

"And Toddy's highchair goes there too."

"Okay," he said.

When we finished, we could see that those few pieces were dwarfed by the large dining space, but at least it looked livable for the time being, and we had a small table to eat on.

"Guess we need a dining table and chairs," Steve said.

"Ya think? When can we buy something? The card table is not very big, and it's getting rickety."

"Maybe next paycheck. That card table doesn't look like it'll take much hard use."

"Wonderful!" I was excited to think that we could start furnishing this large apartment. "I think I'll put the two canvas camp chairs in the foyer. It's a good place to make a little sitting room, don't you think? We can use one of the orange crates as an end table between the two chairs."

We had furnished our student housing apartment in Colorado with inexpensive and hand-me-down pieces. The folding canvas chairs were all we had for seating, except for the two kitchen chairs. Orange crates were great for end tables, nightstands and storage. And they were free, a bonus for students struggling to manage on G.I. Bill benefits.

"Sure," he said as he struggled with our mattress.

I ran to help him with the bed and the two chests of drawers. When we got them installed in the large bedroom, our double bed and small twin dressers looked a bit lost and forlorn. Toddy's crib and dresser also appeared tiny in his large bedroom, filling only one corner of the room. We really did need to get some more furniture.

The third bedroom became a storage room for our suitcases and boxes. A great yawning space led down the long hall, and the living room at the end of the hall would remain empty for the time being. We had more room than furniture.

"I think we need to fill some of those empty spaces, don't you?" I asked.

"As soon as we get some money ahead," Steve promised.

A sizable part of Steve's paycheck that month would go to purchase a dining room set. But where to find one? Hyden had no furniture store, and we discovered that Hazard, twenty-five miles in the other direction, didn't have much choice.

"We can drive to Huntington, West Virginia, next pay day to hunt for what we need," Steve suggested. "It's a big enough town we should be able find something there."

"Great," I said. "How far a drive is it?"

"Not too awfully far, but it will take a long time over those mountain roads. We'll have to spend the night there and come back on Sunday."

"Sounds good to me."

Huntington was the nearest large town, though Lexington, Kentucky, was about the same distance. It *was* a long drive on the winding roads, but a lovely one through the forest with small towns here and there. We had a cranky child by the time we got to Huntington, and we were all glad to get out of the car and walk around the shopping area.

We had hoped to find Danish modern furniture, which we both admired, but after trolling the stores, we found out that not one place had anything modern. Seemed like the mountain natives wanted more traditional styles. We finally settled on a pretty colonial-style, maple table with four chairs and a matching hutch for storage. Although not my first choice, its lovely lines and beautiful wood eventually grew on me.

We also found two very nice maple end tables to replace the orange crates. They had a beautiful finish and simple, clean lines. I'm still using one of them these many years later.

As soon as the furniture was delivered, our family room-kitchen was now habitable. Our new hutch had open shelves above and storage cabinets below. I thoroughly enjoyed filling them up with good dishes and wedding present silver items, all of which had been stored in boxes.

When Steve came home that day, I couldn't wait to show him. "Look! We have furniture! We have a real table to eat on and four chairs to sit on!"

"Hey," he answered. "This looks good. We're going to enjoy this."

"And look at the hutch with all our good dishes on the shelves."

"Very nice," he said. He was never the type to exclaim about things. "And what did you do with the card table and chairs?"

"The card table is in the storage bedroom. One chair is in our bedroom, and the other is in Toddy's room."

"Well, it'll be handy to have a chair to sit on to put on my work boots."

Though he didn't express a whole lot of enthusiasm, Steve enjoyed having the new furniture as much as I did.

We spent most of our time together in the kitchen, cooking and eating or having a cup of coffee and just enjoying each other and our new furniture. I did my sewing on the dining table, and I wrote letters there. Toddy and I visited there while he ate in his highchair. I read a great deal, books and magazines and newspapers, propping them on the new table. The furniture made it feel more like home.

Curtains were the next priority.

"Steve, we really need to have some curtains on these windows. They all face a street. Even though we are up high, I feel so exposed at night with the lights on. People can see inside."

Each bedroom had a large window that opened onto the busy side street, and the living room windows overlooked the parking lot at the front of the store. Even the kitchen windows opened to the road going down to the other homes.

"I suppose that would be a good idea," Steve answered.

"Well, I'll look for fabric next time we go to Hazard and see if I can sew something to cover the windows."

"Okay, Margie," he mumbled. "Sounds good. Whatever you can come up with will be okay."

Curtains were really not his thing.

Fabric was not available at the company store, though they sold almost everything else, from food to tools to hardware to coal. Hazard was the closest town of any size, twenty-five miles away on those mountain roads. We drove up and down the streets to see the shops, a supermarket, doctors, and all the amenities of a medium-sized town.

I finally found curtain fabric in a dry goods store. Back in the apartment, I set up my sewing machine on the table, cut out the fabric, and got to work. It was my first big sewing project, and I learned with each set of curtains.

"Steve, how do you like the curtains I made for the kitchen?"

"Very nice," he said. "Do you want to set up shop and make them to sell?" He was teasing me, of course.

"You're kidding me. These were a lot of work, and I have more windows to go."

By the time I'd finished with the last pair, I was getting pretty proficient. The sewing gave me a yen to do some personal sewing.

Maybe I'd buy some fabric and sew for myself. My wardrobe was pretty skimpy after four years of college with no money for new clothes.

To finish the decorating, we hung a few pictures and bought a couple of throw rugs for the bedrooms and the entryway sitting area. I finally felt settled in our new home. It was a good feeling.

That fall, we learned that my parents planned to come for a visit from Arizona during the Christmas holidays. We had no bed for them, and the empty living room loomed large in our minds.

"What'll we do?" I asked.

"Well, why don't we get a sofa bed to put in the living room? Problem solved—bed and sofa combined!"

"Okay, that's a great idea, but we need more than just a sofa. We need chairs and lamps and a coffee table, and I don't know what else."

"Let me see what I can do about chairs," he said. "I've seen some ads for inexpensive do-it-yourself web chairs. I'll check them out."

After doing his research, Steve bought kits and put together two attractive web chairs, which were surprisingly comfortable. He also built a simple wooden coffee table, varnishing it a light oak color to match the chairs. These were the first of many furniture items that he would build for us over the years.

Toddy "helps" his dad, Steve Conder, put together new web chairs to furnish the living room.

By Christmas, when my parents were due for their visit, we had a hide-a-bed couch in the living room and the two maple end tables we'd gotten in Huntington. The web chairs provided extra seating. The coffee table and a couple of lamps completed the furniture. We hung a few pictures and added a throw rug. The living room was furnished, and my parents were happy in their "guest room."

It was good to have my mom and dad with us for that first Christmas in Kentucky. I hadn't realized how much I missed seeing them. They were happy to see us, too, and loved spending time with Toddy, much changed from six months earlier when they'd seen him last. They also enjoyed getting acquainted with this part of Kentucky where we lived. We celebrated the holiday and hated to see them leave.

However, I felt happy in my own little "nest." I was getting acquainted with the neighbors too. Toddy was growing and developing, walking at last, and beginning to talk a lot. Steve loved his job. Life was good.

Kentucky was becoming home.

CHAPTER 11

Neighbors

"Y'all come in an' set a spell."

This friendly greeting, accompanied by a wide smile flashing two gold eyeteeth, came from my neighbor in the next-door apartment. She was sitting in her hall entryway, door wide open to catch a breeze, fanning herself to keep the muggy heat at bay.

I did go in to "set a spell," and I received a warm welcome from Mrs. McGee, a welcome that lasted for the entire four years we spent in Kentucky.

"Law, I'm mighty pleased to meet you," she said. "I'm Missus McGee. We've been a-wonderin' who was goin' to move in next door. That there's a fine little boy."

"Thank you. We think he's pretty special." I beamed. "I'm pleased to meet you, too. I've been looking forward to getting to know you. I'm Margie, and this is Toddy."

Her friendliness instantly told me I would like her. Tiny but energetic, she was old enough to be my mother, and she would often fill that role with my own mom several thousand miles away. Somehow her lack of education and hill country speech didn't seem important at all. I knew her kindness and sincerity were all that mattered.

The matriarch of a large family of eight children, with four teenagers, two boys and two girls, still at home, Mrs. McGee had plenty to keep her busy. The boys had helped with moving our belongings up those steep stairs. The teenagers were still in school, and all of them would become reliable babysitters for our little boy. Mr. McGee worked as a supervisor in the mine.

I could never call Mrs. McGee by her first name; it seemed disrespectful of someone a generation older than me. She would become a good friend and mentor, and I often went to her for advice. I learned much from her store of practical wisdom about raising babies, cooking southern-style food, and the culture and language of eastern Kentucky. Her lined face reflected a hard life, but those trials had not affected her sweet disposition; they obviously had made her stronger. What a great role model she was!

Often, as I was going in or out of our apartment, I would see Mrs. McGee, sitting in her foyer, fanning her face with a large paper fan and giving me that friendly greeting, "Y'all come in and set a spell." Probably in her mid-fifties at that time, she suffered a great deal that summer from the hot flashes of menopause. The miserable heat and humidity increased her discomfort, so she frequently sat in the entryway to try to catch a bit of moving air.

I often delighted in "setting a spell" with her as she spun her stories about her family and life in Kentucky. It was good to interact with another adult. Steve was gone all day, and though Toddy took up lots of my time as he was learning to walk and talk, I found myself bored with my own company.

One of the McGee's married daughters, Kathleen, lived in the middle apartment tucked in next to ours, with her husband and young daughter. Kathleen, a dark-haired beauty, worked as a clerk in the company store downstairs.

When I first met her, she demonstrated the same sweet disposition as her mother. "I'm Kathleen," she said. "I'm so glad you're our new neighbor." Just like her mother, she radiated warmth even to a furriner like me. "And this is my little girl, Kathy."

"Hi, Kathleen and Kathy. I'm very glad to be your new neighbor, finally! We've been living in the boardinghouse in Hyden for so long that I'd almost given up on meeting anyone here."

"Well, we're glad you're here now."

"How old are you, Kathy?" Her beautiful little daughter was almost a replica of her dark-haired, dark-eyed mom.

"Eight," she answered shyly.

"Well, will you come over and play with Toddy some time?"

"Okay." She smiled.

Kathleen became a warm friend even though she was in her early thirties and I was twenty-one. She worked every day, and I did not see enough of her. As soon as she got off work, she had to come home and fix dinner for her husband and daughter. He worked in the mines, of course, as did all the men in the coal camp. A strong, handsome man, he seemed devoted to his family.

Kathy was a bubbly, friendly little sprite. She knocked on my door one day soon after we moved in. "Can I come play with Toddy today?"

"Of course! Come in. He'll love to have some company." She came in and soon became a precious part of our family.

"How old is he?" she asked.

"Just over a year old."

"How come he's not walking?"

"Well, I guess he needs more practice. Do you want to help?"

"Oh, yes." She beamed.

Tall for his age, Toddy walked late, at 18 months, seeming to find it difficult to balance his long body with his double-jointed knees. (He would grow to be almost six foot six.) Kathy spent endless hours holding his hands to help him walk and sitting on the floor playing with him and his toys. Their favorite game was rolling a soup can down the long hall, which undulated up and down where the floorboards were uneven. He would giggle with delight, and Kathy would laugh and roll it back to him.

"Look what we're doing, Miss Margie." She used the local custom of calling one's elders by their first name, preceded by "Miss" or "Mister" as in "Mister Steve."

"It looks like fun, Kathy."

"Oh, it is so much fun."

They spent many happy hours playing together, and I was grateful to have another child around. I don't think it was only the cookies that lured her to our apartment, but they might have been a temptation.

Some of the McGee's large family lived close by. Besides Kathleen next door, they had another married daughter who lived in the coal camp. She also worked full-time, so I seldom saw her or her husband, but Mrs. McGee would talk to me about all of her children, including two older sons who had moved away from Leslie County and escaped working in the coal mines.

We would enjoy many good times with this delightful family during the years we lived in Kentucky. One memorable occasion was a Halloween party, where we all wore costumes to celebrate the holiday. I made Toddy a little clown suit, complete with pom-poms down the front and a pointed hat. I pulled out of my closet an old Mexican skirt and blouse that I'd bought in Mexico, just across the border from my hometown. Steve wore a bolero over a white shirt with a red sash to look like a real Mexican caballero. I still had a Mexican straw sombrero, so he appeared quite authentic. We were the hit of the party, for they were not familiar with Mexican clothing styles. We had great fun with our new friends that evening and many more times, too.

The McGees exemplified the best of the Kentucky hill folk: honest, hardworking, kind, loving, and caring. Though at that time, many of the local people were unschooled and somewhat ignorant of the rest of the world, it didn't matter to me. I soaked up the wisdom of these wonderful people as well as the stories they told me about the area, the people, their family, and their culture.

I was learning about this part of Kentucky, thanks to the McGees, and I was also learning that a formal education was certainly not necessary to be a good person. These new friends judged me for who I was, and I judged them for who they were, an important lesson for me.

CHAPTER 12

The Company Store

"Do you want a poke?" Kathleen asked the first time I went to the company store to buy groceries.

"What?" I was puzzled. *A poke?*

I'd finished picking out my purchases, and she had gathered them from the shelves and put them on the counter. I hesitated, trying to understand what she meant.

Patiently waiting for my reply, she asked again, "Do you want a poke?"

"I … uh … I … What?" I couldn't envision this sweet woman poking me. Was she joking?

"You want something to carry your groceries with?"

The light finally dawned. "Oh," I said lamely. "Yes, I guess so." *So, a poke is a bag.* I felt foolish, but I had added a new word to my vocabulary. Suddenly I remembered that nursery rhyme about "a pig in a poke." Now it made sense: a pig in a bag. I guess I'd never known what that meant. I was learning more new vocabulary words every day.

The company store was the social center for our small community.

55

In addition to the grocery store, it served as a meeting place, and most times it contained people visiting with one another. Everyone bought their groceries there, paid their bills to the company for rent and food and coal, and picked up their wages and the mail in that building. It was a busy place.

One day, when I went down to buy a few groceries, I was amazed to see, parked in front of the store, a mule hitched up to a large wooden sled.

"Look, Toddy! A mule and a sled!" I said.

He toddled over to the sled, which had steel runners to navigate the dirt trails. Toddy grinned at me as he began to explore the sled and then moved on toward the mule. I picked him up quickly since I had no idea if the mule might object to his curiosity.

"That's a mule, Toddy. Like a horse." He had seen pictures of horses in some of his books.

"Horsey?"

"No, a mule. *Like* a horsey."

"Moo?"

"Close enough." I laughed.

Just then, a man came out of the store with several bags over his shoulder and a sack, er, poke, full of other groceries. He headed for the sled, and I realized he was going to pack it with his purchases They included bags of flour and sugar and a large sack of dried pinto beans, probably just the staples he couldn't produce himself on his small farm. No fresh vegetables or fruit or canned goods, but interestingly enough, a large box of corn flakes. I guessed that some modern things had gained popularity up in the hills.

Seeing the man loading his sled with just the bare necessities, I learned something about how simply the local people lived. It was an awakening for me to see how hard life was for them, having to raise most of their food, living up in the hills and hollers with no real roads. People had probably been living like that for any number of generations. It could not have been easy. Fortunately, this man had a mule to haul the iron-runner sled for transportation.

The incident vividly illustrated the contrast between modern life as

I knew it then in 1951 and the lives of those hill people who populated this rural county. The natives had lived a hardscrabble existence before the mines opened, and it was still a difficult life unless the men worked in the mines.

However, the hill-dwellers were self-sufficient; they had to be. I learned that most farmed their hillside plots, raising corn and chickens, a pig or two for meat and lard and possibly a cow, and growing vegetables in their gardens and fruit from their trees. Where I had bought frozen orange juice, bakery bread, canned vegetables and bottled vegetable oil at the store, this man had purchased only the basic supplies to bake his own bread and the pinto beans that provided the backbone of his family's meals. He had little need for modern civilization and probably lived much as his ancestors had.

Except for the corn flakes, of course!

CHAPTER 13

The Still

Zip, zip, zip.

The buzzing sounds swished over the top of Steve's head, but he paid no attention to them. He was concentrating on his work at the transit, gathering data for his survey. He and his helpers had climbed the heavily wooded hillside on a hot summer day to check out some boundaries of the coal company's property.

Hard at work, mining engineer Steve Conder has his head down over his surveying transit.

Steve's brush cutter, Pleazy Sizemore, had hacked at the thick underbrush with brush hooks and machetes to open a clearing for the transit reading. The surveying helper, Mark Sizemore, had carried the chain up the steep hill while Steve followed with the transit. Mark and Pleazy were not closely related, but in that area, which had been isolated for so many years, most people were "kinfolk," even distantly, and many carried the same surname.

Sweat poured off their faces as the men worked, and they swatted at the insects buzzing noisily around them. Finally, a large enough opening cut in the brush allowed a clear line of sight to use the transit and chain.

"Looking good," Steve told his helpers as he bent over the transit. Absorbed in his calculations, Steve was not fully aware of his surroundings. When the zip, zip, zip went over his head, he ignored it. Bees, perhaps?

He was oblivious for a second or two until Pleazy shouted, "Mistuh Steve! Mistuh Steve!" He came half-running and half-sliding down the hill, his voice frantic, his face anxious.

"What?" Steve looked up, irritated at the interruption.

Breathless, Pleazy gasped, "Mistuh Steve, we gotta get outta here *raht now!*"

"Why? What's the matter?"

"We'uns got too close to somebody's still," Pleazy said. "And they's a-shootin' at us!" The thick underbrush had muffled the bang of the gun, but Pleazy and Mark knew what the zip, zip, zip meant, having grown up in the mountains, where everyone had guns and shootings were common. The sounds of the bullets passing overhead sent a clear warning. The men had penetrated deep into the forest, coming too close to a hidden still.

Steve got the message. "Let's go *now!*" He hoisted the transit over his shoulder while Mark and Pleazy quickly picked up the rest of the gear.

The three men slipped and slid down the hill in record time.

When they got back to their truck, Pleazy heaved a sigh of relief. "Them shots was just a warnin'. They coulda killed us daid if they'd a-wanted to." His voice trembled a bit.

"Well, thank goodness they're good shots," said Steve, trying to lighten the mood. "At least they missed us!"

Mark and Pleazy laughed. Now that they were safe, this would be a great story to tell their friends and families. Steve laughed with them, relieved to have put some distance between his crew and the moonshiner.

"But we still have to get that area surveyed," Steve said. "We've got to go back there."

"That's okay," said Pleazy. "We kin go back thar in a week or so, and hit'll be safe. They'll move that ole still raht away, now that we know where it's at."

Pleazy was right. When the men returned several weeks later, they climbed the hill warily, but the woods were quiet. They heard only the buzzing insects and the gentle rustle of leaves in the breeze. The still was gone, relocated somewhere else far away.

Steve chuckled as he told me about the shooting that night, but I didn't laugh. I didn't find it the least bit humorous that someone had shot at my husband, warning or not. It was a vivid lesson to me that the Kentucky mountain men didn't hesitate to use the guns they carried.

Gunfire would continue to punctuate our four-year stay in eastern Kentucky. Every man carried a gun in the "olden" days, not that many years before we arrived in the summer of 1951. Most still did. Guns had been a necessity for these people living in the mountains, isolated for several hundred years until World War II opened up the area in the search for much-needed coal. Lawmen were far away, and men used guns for self-protection, for hunting, to solve disputes, and even for prestige.

By the time we arrived, ten years later, good-paying jobs in the coal mines had improved the lives of many of those hardy descendants of the early settlers by providing them with much-needed cash. However, as we would learn, their way of life, their philosophy, their language, and their reliance on their guns had actually changed very little.

CHAPTER 14

More Gunfire

Crash! Bang! Crack!

We awakened with a startle in the middle of the night.

"What on earth?" I asked.

"Oh, it's just the pipes in the attic falling again," Steve said sleepily. Several weeks earlier, the pipes in the attic carrying steam to our radiators had fallen from their supports with a similar loud crash. So, we turned over and went back to sleep.

In the morning, we went downstairs to report the pipes' falling, and we discovered it wasn't the pipes that had caused the crashing. All the large plate glass windows of the storefront were shattered, and broken glass was all over the ground and inside the store. The loud noise we'd heard in the night had obviously been the windows breaking. Luckily, our living room windows on the second floor above the broken ones were still intact. Nevertheless, it was frightening to have such violence perpetrated so close to home.

"Steve, the store windows are all gone."

"Another shooting, I guess," he answered calmly.

I wasn't so calm. "Look how close to our windows this shooting was! If we'd been in the living room, we might have been in danger."

"Not to worry, honey," he said. "They only shot out those store windows to send a message to the coal company from some angry union members. They're upset that the employees of our coal company are still resisting their being organized. Union organizers are still trying to convince the nonunion miners working for our coal company to join." He sighed. "When will they learn that most of our miners don't want the union here? Of course," Steve added with a grin, "it could have been someone tanked up on moonshine who just couldn't resist knocking out those big plate glass windows."

Though Leslie County was a dry county, where liquor could not be sold legally, moonshine was readily available for anyone who wished to have a drink of "likker." We had learned about illegal stills when Steve and his helpers were warned away from one. The easy availability of illegal alcohol and the pervasive number of guns often led to violence, which was sometimes deadly.

At the gas station up the hill, a person could buy *gallons* of gas and *quarts* or *pints* of "white lightnin'." We heard enough stories about the adverse physical effects of drinking this potent, high-octane moonshine that we never tried any, preferring to purchase what little liquor we wanted in nearby Hazard. In Perry County, selling alcohol was legal and was safe to drink.

Most people assumed that the shooting out the store windows was union violence rather than a random shoot-'em-up.

"Either way, it reminds me that so many men here carry guns, and they use them," I said. "Remember the first day I arrived in Hyden? Those men and their guns frightened me to death."

Though we'd not seen much violence since we'd moved to the coal camp, until that morning, the threat still stalked the hills and hollers nearby. We often heard of shootings back in the hollers, bad blood between families. It hadn't been all that many years since guns took care of most differences between people, and even though the county now had a sheriff and deputies, some people still settled their arguments with bullets. We didn't live too far from the area where the Hatfields and the McCoys had feuded and killed each other.

Luckily, the shooting incident was not repeated, but the perpetrators were never caught.

Steve learned about another act of local gun violence from his surveying helper, Pleazy Sizemore. A local man, Pleazy's brother-in-law, had recently been shot to death in the area where Steve and Pleazy were surveying up in the hills.

They stopped by a creek to eat their lunch, and while they were eating, Pleazy said, "You know, Mistuh Steve, if a fella was to sit right beside that there rock, he could draw a bead on someone's haid as he walked down that trail ... and shoot him daid."

When Pleazy said those words, Steve gulped. The brother-in-law was known to be physically abusive to Pleazy's sister, and the shooting put a stop to the beatings. It seemed that Pleazy knew a bit too much about the shooting site. Steve said nothing, but he wandered over to the rock where he found a spent shell just at the spot where Pleazy had said someone could "draw a bead on someone's haid." Was he hinting that he had shot his brother-in-law?

Evidently, the sheriff thought that Pleazy had done it. He had plenty of motive, and he was soon arrested, indicted, and tried on murder charges. When the verdict came in, the jury found him not guilty. In hill country justice, the shooting was justified. It put a stop to the physical abuse of Pleazy's sister. In those days, it seemed that a justified murder was less heinous even than stealing, which was considered a far more serious crime. We learned that this attitude, which I found surprising, was commonly accepted among the local people at that time.

As Mary Breckinridge wrote in her book, *Wide Neighborhoods,* in Leslie County, "An example of their pioneer code is that stealing is held to be a greater crime than shooting an enemy."[1] She had lived in Leslie County for more than twenty-five years and knew the local people well.

Fortunately, we were personally spared the violence still simmering

[1] Mary Breckinridge, *Wide Neighborhoods* (New York: Harper & Brothers, 1952) p. 170

in the county, but my awareness of the possibility of its occurring never left my mind during the entire four years we lived there. A small nagging fear jumped to the surface whenever we heard of a shooting or tragic gunshot accident. With plenty of bootleg liquor readily to ignite passions, it's a wonder we didn't have even more cases of deadly violence.

It was just a fact of life in Leslie County in the 1950s.

CHAPTER 15

A New Language

Soon after we'd moved into the apartment, Mrs. McGee said, "I'll be over this evenin' after dinner." Delighted to entertain my first visitor, I decided to make something to serve when she came. As soon as I put Toddy down for his afternoon nap, I got out the ingredients to make oatmeal cookies, our family favorite. I was in the middle of stirring up the batter when I heard a knock on the door.

Who could that be? Right after lunch?

I wiped my floury hands clean and opened the door to see Mrs. McGee. Surprised to see her then instead of after dinner, I stumbled over my welcome. "Come in, come in. I just didn't expect you so soon."

"But I told you I'd be over this evenin' after dinner," she said.

"Yes, but—" I suddenly realized that *her* evenin' and dinner and *mine* were not the same.

Dinner is the midday meal in the hill country, and indeed in most of the South, I learned. So, everything after dinner is evenin'. The evening meal is supper. The word *lunch* was unheard of.

Mrs. McGee just chuckled at my misunderstanding, and we settled down for a visit. I took her the cookies later. It was not my first lesson in this new language, but I never forgot it. I already had learned *crick* and *holler* and *branch* and *poke*, but the words regarding mealtimes were far more important to understand.

I was just digesting the use of the word *poke* when Mrs. McGee told me she was making *poke sallet* for dinner. What on earth? I discovered that *poke* is also a generic term used for all kinds of wild greens, and *poke sallet* is a salad made from those greens.

Thus began my real education in the fascinating language of the hill country. Much of this language is common everywhere in the South, but it was all new to me as a westerner who was ignorant of the local usage. An English major in college who loved to write, I thought I had a pretty good vocabulary, but it was expanding rapidly.

Learning colorful new words intrigued me. Mrs. McGee taught me many unfamiliar expressions, which soon became familiar, as I listened to her and to other Kentucky friends when they spoke.

Y'all is pretty self-explanatory, usually indicating one person, while *all y'all* is the plural form. Even after many years away from the South, I find myself using *y'all* frequently. It's just a comfortable expression, easy on the tongue.

Reckon had to be a word I heard every day. Used instead of "guess" or "suppose," it had a lovely southern sound.

"I *reckon* I'll go."

"Does she *reckon* he'll come?"

"Do you *reckon* it's gonna rain?"

The word *law* seemed to be a good introductory word for many sentences.

"*Law*, can you believe that!"

"*Law*, I never thought I'd see the day!"

"*Law almighty*, it's hot today!" The "almighty" added emphasis. I soon found that usage in my vocabulary too.

One word I never could manage to say was *ain't*, so frequently spoken by the local people. Avoiding this word had been drilled firmly into me from childhood, and I couldn't even say it. But I heard it all the time, singular or plural, sort of a combination of *isn't* and *aren't*.

"He *ain't* coming."

"They *ain't* going.

Cain't, meaning cannot, was another word I heard so often that I didn't even blink an eye.

"I *cain't* go today."

"He *cain't* run fast."

"They *cain't* do that."

This was also a word I just couldn't put my tongue around. *Can't* was what automatically came out of my mouth.

Sometimes it would be *tain't*, a contraction for the negative "it ain't," as in "*tain't* the truth."

"*Mam-maw, Mam-maw*, where are you?" Little Kathy taught me the Kentucky version for grandmother, which sounds sort of like "Grandma," as she would run to the McGees' apartment. My grandmother was just "Grandmother," and my friends had "grandmas" or "nanas." *Mam-maw*, however, sounded perfect, and I was charmed by hearing it.

And when Kathy said, "*Pap-paw*, I love you," I learned the southern word for grandfather. Having read many historical novels set in England, I know that *Mam* and *Pap* were common terms for one's parents in previous times; by extension, *Mam-maw* and *Pap-paw* sound logical to call one's grandparents.

Kinfolks, uttered so often, told me a lot about family ties; close ties made people *kin*. Seemed like everyone in Leslie County were *kin*; those many years of isolation meant that families intermarried frequently.

"I'm goin' to *carry* my mother to town" sounded strange to me the first time a friend said it to me. I had this vivid picture of my acquaintance picking up her overweight mother, throwing her over her shoulder with a great deal of difficulty, and actually carrying her to town. It didn't take long for me to realize the word was a substitute for "take," but I still chuckled inside every time I heard it.

"Give me some *sugah*" had become a familiar expression to me when our Hyden landlady picked up our baby son and asked for a kiss. Mrs. McGee also used this word often when she saw our Toddy or her own granddaughter. That's one common southern usage that I love. *Sugah* aptly connotes the sweetness of a kiss.

"I'm *a-fixin'* to start supper."

"I'm *a-fixin'* to go to town."

We heard this word combination every day. *A-fixin'* seemed useful to show that one was ready to do something and far more colorful than just "going to" do something.

Light bread, commonly spoken by the local people, confused me at first. What was *light bread*, anyway? I was to learn that is the term for an ordinary store-bought loaf of bread. I conjectured that if some bread was "light," then was there a "dark" bread? But, no, biscuits and corn bread, the other breads commonly eaten in hill country, are called by their own names.

"Her *misries* are a-keepin' her in bed," Mrs. McGee told me one day. That one I could figure out since it is so close to "miseries." Still, *misries* sounded so much worse.

Warshing was such a common usage that I paid little attention to it, though I couldn't bring myself to put the "r" in the word "washing." But it painted a vivid picture in my mind of the old-fashioned washboards.

While many new words began to fill my speech, I was also learning different pronunciations for familiar words. Some of my initial confusion with the mountain language arose from the differences, but I soon learned to understand and use the local variations. It didn't take long to get into the swing of the hill country accent. Hearing others' speech patterns has an insidious way of insinuating those same patterns into one's own usage, and I quickly picked up on the local ones by just listening to the native speakers.

Every word that ended in "ing" dropped the G. "We're goin' to town." "It's rainin' today." "The crick's runnin' high." It didn't take me long to adopt that soft, lazy pronunciation. To this day, I have to concentrate to put a G on the end of an "ing" word, which was a bit embarrassing years later when I was teaching high school English classes.

It was only when we talked to my parents on the phone that I heard myself drawling out one-syllable words into two syllables and saying *I reckon so* or *y'all*. I know I had developed a typical Kentucky twang to my speech when we went back West four years later.

One of the most surprising aspects about the speech of the area was that so many of the local people were actually speaking what sounded like Elizabethan English. Having studied Shakespeare and Elizabethan drama in college, I was somewhat familiar with the dialect of those plays written so many years ago. However, I'd heard it spoken only in the plays I'd seen—and certainly not as the everyday language of the people. The first time I heard someone speak of the *yarbs* (herbs) they used as medicines, I heard Shakespeare's voice. When someone said he was *afeared* of the dark, I heard Elizabethan speech. The cadence, phrasing, and vocabulary of the local people all rang a familiar bell in my mind.

When I learned that the hills and hollers of that part of Kentucky had been isolated from the rest of the United States for several hundred years, I discovered the reason for their using two hundred-year-old English. Those British settlers who followed Daniel Boone on the "Wilderness Trail" in the 1700s brought their language with them, and they were still using it when we arrived in 1951. A few of the local people still had land grants from the king of England to show title to their property as they had settled there before the American Revolution.

In their remote mountain communities, kept apart from the rest of the country by the steep and heavily wooded terrain, many families intermarried, and they kept their language, their customs, and their culture for those many years until World War II in the 1940s brought modern civilization into their isolated lives.

Many years later, when I read Mary Breckinridge's delightful story of the Frontier Nursing Service, which she founded and ran for many years, I appreciated her comment about the local speech, which confirmed my thinking:

> The Highlanders remained out of touch because of their extreme inaccessibility ... (so) the customs and language of an earlier Anglo-Saxon age continued to flow ... All sorts of lovely words of Chaucerean and Shakespearean descent remained in use ... [2]

---

[2] Ibid, p. 170

Every day brought new words that seemed strange to me, and I soon was relishing the richness of the mountain speech. I discovered that those regional and local differences added a great deal of color to our American English. I not only enjoyed this new language, but as I began to use it on a regular basis, I was beginning to fit in. Nothing marked us as furriners more than using our western speech patterns. So, we adapted, and it wasn't too hard since the local speech was all we heard.

CHAPTER 16

New Friends

During our daily visits to the company store Toddy and I soon became acquainted with other neighbors in the coal camp. We went there every day to pick up mail and groceries. Hauling a poke of groceries and a heavy baby up those steep stairs to our apartment meant that I shopped for only a few items at a time.

When I first met Grace, I had no idea that she would become a dear friend.

"You must be our new neighbor," she said to me as I was getting my groceries. "I'm Grace Franks, and I live in the house by the bridge."

"I'm so glad to meet you," I said. "It's good to meet our neighbors."

"You must come see me," she said with a lovely smile. "You and that sweet little boy." She gave Toddy a gentle pat on the arm.

"I'd love to," I said.

She and Clyde lived in one of the brick homes across the street from the miners' houses. Their brick house sat right on the edge of Cutshin Creek. When I knocked on the door that first time, Grace immediately made us feel welcome.

"Y'all come right in," she said, smiling. She had a cookie for Toddy and a cup of coffee for me. We visited and got acquainted a bit, and she was to become a great friend as well as neighbor.

Grace and Clyde were staunch Southern Baptists, as were many of the locals, and they were honest and moral, good people. Although their children were grown, Grace took a fancy to Toddy and invited us to visit her, partly I think, to dote on the baby.

Later on, when the first television service arrived in the coal camp, Grace graciously invited us to come over to share in this marvelous invention. Three-year-old Toddy would go to their house every morning to watch *Romper Room*, a special show aired for pre-schoolers. I don't know who enjoyed that more––Toddy or Grace.

The Franks were to prove their friendship over and over, in many ways, whether it was with the gift of some wonderful, edible treat, just a visit to chat, or even sharing their home with us when ours became uninhabitable in the middle of an ice storm.

Another neighbor and his wife were the boss's brother, Jim, and his wife, Jean. He was the business manager of the company, including the store and office. They also lived in one of the brick homes backing up to Cutshin Crick. I met Jean at the company store, too. She was a superb cook, and her desserts were to die for. Warm and jolly, she twinkled as she talked and was a wonderful advertisement for her cooking skills. We felt privileged to enjoy delicious meals at their home.

I still use some of Jean's recipes, especially for her mouth-watering cakes and her delicious barbecue sauce. Growing up in the West, I thought that beef barbecue was the only kind to have. I was soon to learn the delights of southern pork barbecue, coated with Jean's lovely barbecue sauce.

Several months after we moved into the coal camp, we got acquainted another new couple. Steve came home with an invitation from his boss, Mack Smith, the coal company owner.

"Mack wants us to come to dinner," he said. "Next Sunday."

"Really? That's so nice. What's the big occasion?"

"I think it's just because he and my dad are friends." Steve's father was a friend of the Smiths, having called on Mack often in his job of buying coal for his firm. Now that Steve's dad was retired and living in Florida, the Smiths had visited them there. So, though we were not too surprised to receive the dinner invitation, it was exciting to be invited to their home.

"I'll have to get a babysitter."

"No, Toddy is included."

"Wow, that's good. Sounds like they want to meet him too."

I was a bit nervous as the time approached. I'd not met Mrs. Smith and had spoken to Mack only a few times, very briefly, so it would be the first time to get acquainted. I was enjoying getting acquainted with more people, but meeting the boss and his family was a very big deal.

"What will I wear?" I asked Steve. The eternal question asked by wives.

"Whatever you want, Margie. You always look nice."

So helpful he was.

My small wardrobe consisted mostly of pants, skirts and tops and a few casual dresses, but I found a nice dress from my college days deep in the back of my closet and was glad to dress up a bit for the first time since we'd been in Kentucky. I was hoping to make a good impression. I even wore earrings.

"How do I look?" I posed for Steve to see.

"You look great, honey," he said, giving me a kiss on the top of my head.

"Do you think this outfit is okay for dinner with your boss?"

"Absolutely."

"Then let's be off so we aren't late."

"We're on our way now."

Thus assured, I felt I was up to meeting the boss and his wife, though it might be a bit scary.

The twenty-five-mile drive to Hazard was scary, too. It took forty-five minutes to an hour, with our speed regulated by tight curves and huge coal trucks barreling down the road in each direction, often heading straight at us on our side of the road. I always heaved a sigh of relief when we arrived safely in town.

A lovely welcome awaited us when we arrived at the Smiths' home.

"I'm so happy to meet you both," Mrs. Smith said, smiling as she invited us in. "And this is your precious little boy." She was a charming southern lady, who made us feel right at home. Mac, too, was a hospitable host. The dinner was delicious, and the presence of their daughter, close to my age, made the evening even more pleasant.

Before we left, they presented us with a delightful surprise: a lovely maple Windsor chair with a cane seat.

"This is a belated wedding present," Mrs. Smith said. They'd been on our wedding invitation list several years earlier because of their being friends with Steve's dad and stepmother.

"How beautiful!" I was overwhelmed; the gift was completely unexpected. "Thank you so much.," I said. "You are so kind to do this." We happily added the chair to our few pieces of furniture, and I'm still loving it many years later.

On the way home, I said, "It was good to get acquainted with your boss and his wife."

"I'm glad you got to meet them. They are really nice people. I respect my boss; he is a great businessman who seems to care about all his employees."

"Well, I guess we are lucky that you are working for him."

"You are so right."

Though they were not neighbors and Mack was Steve's boss, I felt that after the lovely reception they gave us, I could count them as new friends.

Looking back on those years in the coal camp, I find that some of our happiest times were sitting with good people around a dining table, enjoying the fruits of someone's expert southern cooking. To this day, I remember with deep gratitude those friendly people who welcomed us to their small community with kindness and southern hospitality. They epitomized the best of eastern Kentucky.

CHAPTER 17

The Warshin'

My kitchen window gave us a glimpse into the lives of those other neighbors who lived behind the store.

"Look, Steve, at how many of those little houses on the hill have big Cadillacs parked out in front of their homes." We were still driving a twelve-year-old Chevrolet, but we hoped to replace it once we saved up the money. It had replaced our first car, a vintage 1936, which had broken down on Steve's eventful trip hauling all our worldly goods from Denver to Kentucky. He had been able to buy the Chevy on credit from an angel of a car dealer in Hill City, Kansas. Though Steve had no money to pay for it that day, the dealer had accepted a postdated check after learning he was just about to start his job in Kentucky. We felt fortunate to have our old car, which was reliable transportation, but it paled in comparison with the Cadillacs.

"These miners are making good money," Steve said, "and they want people to know it. They probably never had a car, much less an expensive one, when they were living up in the hills before the mines opened. So, it's sort of a status symbol."

"Oh, so that's why they all have expensive cars," I said. "When you have lived in poverty for many years, it must feel good to be able to buy a car. And especially a luxury car."

"That's for sure," Steve answered.

"And why do they all have washing machines on the front porch?" I'd seen them from the kitchen window too.

"Another status symbol," my husband said.

"Well, I can understand that."

The electric washing machine was a vast improvement over the washboards used by the mountain women up in the hills who had no electricity, and the miners' wives in the coal camp were proud to own them and show them off. However, I learned that it was still a huge job for the coal camp women to do the *warshin'*.

One day, I glanced out my kitchen window to see our closest neighbor on the hill, Mrs. Browning, starting to do her laundry with the help of some of her many children. With my kitchen window open that summer day, I could hear her conversation.

"Hurry up, then, git the fire started," she told her oldest boy.

Fascinated, I watched her son build a fire on the ground near the water spigot outside the kitchen door. A big, black galvanized washtub sat over the fire on rocks. Mrs. Browning, with the help of her children, filled it with water from the spigot, bucketful by bucketful, to heat over the open fire. No wonder the washtub was black.

When the water was hot, she and the children carried it, bucketful by bucketful again, up six or seven steps to the front porch to fill the washing machine. Then they put the soap and dirty laundry in to wash.

While the laundry was swishing around in the washing machine, they were hauling more buckets of water to heat over the fire for rinsing. After the clothes were washed clean, Mrs. Browning put them through the wringer, rinsed them in the clean water in the washtub, and then ran them through the wringer again.

"Hang them clothes up," Mrs. Browning told her daughters.

The girls hung them to dry on bushes and the porch railing and on a rope hung below on the porch supports. Then they repeated the cycle until all the laundry for a family with seven children was finished.

Oh, those wringers did beat wringing the clothes out by hand, and the washing machine beat the washboard, but doing the laundry was still a lot of work. Thank goodness, Mrs. Browning had a big family to help. When I saw what a huge job doing laundry was for my neighbor, I counted my blessings that my wringer washer in the corner of the kitchen was hooked up to a hot water tap. Even though doing my laundry was a chore, it hardly compared to what she had to do.

The miners' homes were pretty primitive, I found out. Everyone had a coal cookstove and a fireplace, but no furnace. The women had to build a fire in the stove to cook their meals, even on the hottest summer days. Of course, it helped heat the house in the winter, too. Every stove had a big teakettle simmering at the back, which supplied hot water for cooking or bathing. This was not too different from what these women had up in the hollers, so they seemed to take it for granted, but I admired them as I knew how much effort it must take just to do everyday housework.

How would I have fared if I were plunked down in one of these homes? Hmmm. Probably not too well. I grew up in a home with all modern conveniences, especially an indoor bathroom with flush toilet and big bathtub to soak in. It would have been quite an adjustment then; however, I did learn to handle similar cooking conditions many years later when we had a cabin in the Arizona mountains with no running water and only a woodstove and fireplace to provide for most of the cooking and heat. I thought about the families in the coal camp then.

Fortunately, our apartment over the company store had all the amenities: indoor plumbing, electricity, a hot-water heater, and furnace heat. It was a real eye-opener for me to see the daily difficulties of life that these hill women faced. How lucky was I! And thinking of the women who lived up in the hills without either electricity or running water made me even more aware of my good fortune.

However, I would come to envy their more primitive lifestyle several years later when a three-day power outage in the middle of an icy snowstorm meant we had no heat, no lights, and no way to cook meals while the miners' families could cook and stay comfortably warm with their coal stoves and fireplaces.

These neighbors and new friends all helped me grow in knowledge of Appalachia culture and proved to be of great importance in my new Kentucky life. Though their way of life was far different from that which I'd known growing up, as I learned more about Kentucky, I began to appreciate those things that made this part of the country so special.

More importantly, I learned to appreciate the best qualities of these mountain folk. In spite of their lack of education, these were hard-working, intelligent people who had much to teach me. I know I learned much from each of them, including a large dose of humility. No longer did I think I knew everything, with my college education and Phi Beta Kappa key. I discovered many more important life lessons than contained in my college textbooks.

The college degree I so prized counted for little in our new home. I was a furriner in a strange country, growing in knowledge as I learned the different ways of a different people, good people, honest, independent and made strong by coping with many hardships of life. I appreciated these new friends for all they had to teach me and for their caring, their acceptance, and their kindness to us. My values were changing as I realized that an education was not at all essential to becoming a good, productive human being.

CHAPTER 18

The Coal Mine

The mining company for which Steve worked operated three or four small nonunion coal mines. The largest one, where he spent most of his time, was cut into a steep hillside not far from the coal camp where we lived. Each mine was different, of course, but in general, the underground operations were similar. In the 1950s, in eastern Kentucky, all of the mines that the company owned were underground properties; the open-pit mines that so scarred the lovely mountains would arrive years later.

Smith Coaal Mine #1 and tipple sit on the side of a Leslie County mountainside.

I knew nothing about coal mining when we came to Kentucky. I knew a bit about copper mining because my dad had worked for a copper mining company in Arizona, but underground coal mining is far different, as I was to learn.

One day, I took Steve to work so I could use the car. I'd never been to the mine site.

As we drove the dirt road up the mountainside to the mine, I could see several buildings situated on a level plot of land, a bench cut into the slope of the hill.

"What are all those buildings?" I asked.

"This first one is the superintendent's shack, but it's not just for the superintendent. The miners check in their guns in the shack because guns are not allowed underground." Many of the miners carried their weapons with them at all times, except when they were working.

"I should hope not! Just imagine what might happen if a gunfight broke out deep in the mine. What are those other buildings?"

"One is the lamp house, and the others are maintenance and storage buildings. See those men going into the lamp house? They are picking up their battery-operated headlamps that they wear on their hard hats underground. They also get their personal brass tags and hang them on a board to show they are in the mine today, sort of like punching a time clock. When the tags are hung on the board, supervisors can keep track of who is working today. At the end of the shift, each man takes his tag off the board and turns it in. A tag left on the board means a missing man."

"Wow! It's good they can keep track of each man."

The sight of the men gathered at the mine before their day's work presented an unforgettable picture. Dressed in coveralls tightly taped at ankles and wrists to keep out the coal dust and work boots into which their pant legs were tucked, the miners wore hard hats with battery-operated lamps attached to give them light while underground.

Each man carried a round, metal lunch bucket, about ten inches high, with a wire handle. Steve was the only one to have an ordinary rectangular lunch box that he'd brought with us from Colorado. The miners ate their lunches underground, sitting on the floor of the mine, but usually had no other breaks.

Steve pointed to the two large half-circle openings that cut into the side of the hill to mark the mine entrance. The wide-open mouths, about eighteen to twenty feet across, appeared big enough to drive a truck through.

"Those openings are called adits," said Steve, "and that first one is where the men go into the mine. It has conveyer belts that we ride on to go in and come back out. The belts also bring out the coal from deep in the mine."

Steve Conder watches the conveyor belt bringing out coal from inside the Mary Gail #3 mine.

"What's the other one for?"

"The other one has a huge exhaust fan, which pulls air into the mine tunnels from the first adit and then out through that exhaust fan in the second adit. Without it, we wouldn't have any fresh air."

The horizontal tunnels that contained the seams of coal extended so far into the hillside that without the exhaust fan pulling air inside, the miners would not have enough oxygen to breathe.

"What happens if the power goes out?" I asked, visualizing the men underground with no fresh air.

"We have generators to back up the power. But even with the

powerful blower, there's always the danger of not enough oxygen and a buildup of carbon monoxide. I get a ping in the middle of the forehead that warns me if the air gets bad. That's my signal that we need to get out fast."

I cringed a little at that thought, but I didn't say anything to Steve. He knew I was a worrier, so there was no need to mention it.

Sensing my discomfort, Steve said, "This company is very safety conscious. Before we go in, the fire boss starts the day by checking all the workplaces for explosive methane gas. He also checks the safety of the ceiling, called the 'back,' of each entry or tunnel. The fire boss's job is dangerous. He might find methane, which could explode with even a tiny spark caused by metal on metal. If the ceiling is bad, it might fall on him as he tests it. If he finds everything is in order and relatively safe, then the miners can go in for their day's work. They pay the fire boss very well for the danger he faces every day.

"The coal dust itself is another danger that the company guards against. It is easily ignited by a stray spark. So, each day, the workings are treated with rock dust to coat the area and cut down the risk of an explosion and fire. Safety for the men is always a big concern. That's why they check everything before we go in."

I was glad to hear of all the safety precautions, but none of his information had allayed my fears about his working in an underground coal mine.

Yet I found it fascinating to learn something about the coal mining process as it was practiced at this mine, which was almost completely mechanized. As Steve told me what a typical day was like, I tried to imagine the scene underground.

The tunnels in this mine were so low that a man could not stand upright. They would ride the conveyor belt, kneeling all the way to the coal face, where the black mineral was being extracted. The entries, tunnels which had already been excavated, were propped up with heavy timbers on the sides and across the top. Pillars of coal were also left at intervals to help provide support for the ceilings.

The 3-foot high seam of coal is exposed at the groundbreaking for Mary Gail #3 mine. Men could not stand up in mines this low.

First, a machine would undercut the face of the coal, so that it would fall where it could easily be shoveled up. The drillers drilled holes for the explosives in a preset pattern to show what area was to be cut. They used high-pressure compressed gas cylinders to break the coal away from the seam, which was considerably safer than dynamite. Before they set it off, the face boss would make sure that all men were clear of the area.

After the explosion blew the coal from the face to the floor, the miners had to load it into a shuttle railcar, or "buggy," that took it to the surface. The mechanized mines like this one had a loading machine to scrape up the broken coal pieces onto a conveyor and then into the waiting buggy. In other mines, the men had to shovel it up manually, a tough job when they couldn't even stand up to work.

When the buggy was full of coal, another one would come in to receive its load. The loaded cars were driven to a hopper at the loading station, where the coal was loaded onto the conveyor belt and out to the surface. Then the whole process was repeated again and again.

After his description, Steve got out of the car, put on his hard hat, and went to get his tag and headlamp. I watched as the men chatted together, smoking and waiting to enter the mine. When it came time to go to work, the miners put out their cigarettes, which could easily start a fire underground, and knelt on the conveyor belt that took them deep into the mine.

It was quite a process, bringing the coal up from the bowels of the earth to fuel the factories and heat the homes of countless people. The more I learned about the coal mining process, the more respect I had for these miners. They worked so hard under such dangerous conditions at physically challenging jobs for twenty-five dollars a day. That was a fair wage in 1951, but no amount of money could persuade some people to do it. The young men in the county looked elsewhere for jobs, and many of them headed to Ohio where they could find safer work.

When I went back that afternoon to pick up Steve, I saw the weary men, black with coal dust, riding the conveyor belt back out. Then they went into the lamp house to replace their headlamps to be recharged for the next day, took their brass tags off the board, and retrieved their guns before they went home. I'll always remember that indelible picture.

When Steve got back in the car, he pointed out huge coal trucks lined up to receive the coal. "Those trucks take the coal to the tipple in Hazard, where they load it into train cars. From there, trains take it to the buyers."

Coal trucks fill their load from the tipple at Smith #1 mine, heading to the train tipple in Hazard.

The narrow, winding highway between the mine and Hazard at that time was treacherous. The huge, heavily loaded trucks went speeding around the curves—often on the wrong side of the road. The empty trucks coming back for another load were especially dangerous since they were capable of more speed than the loaded ones, and the truck drivers were always in a hurry to get back for another load, another paycheck. The road was considered so dangerous that State Farm canceled our auto insurance, and we had to find another company to insure our car. To this day, Steve drives at the far-right side of every road, almost off the pavement, a habit made necessary by those speeding coal trucks in Kentucky.

Underground coal mining is hard, dirty, and inherently dangerous work, and the men who work underground are brave souls who face that danger every day. Explosions, fires, deadly gas, and slate falls are only some of the occupational hazards for underground miners. Unstable roofs and buildups of methane gas that can cause explosions are real possibilities, and working with explosives underground can be a dicey proposition.

Steve came home one day to tell me about another danger. He looked worried. "We've got a fire in the mine today." Fires in the mines were not uncommon, with so many hazardous sources of ignition.

"That's not good," I said. "What started it?"

"Probably a short in some of the machinery."

"Is anyone hurt?" I asked.

"Luckily, no," he answered. "No men were trapped behind the fire; if they had been, the chances of their surviving would be next to nothing. But we had to wall off the fire from the rest of the mine to cut off the oxygen which feeds it. The men built brattices to do that. Hopefully that will put out the fire."

Brattices are solid walls, built from the floor to the roof of the mine, filling the whole tunnel, in order to wall off the fire and keep oxygen from getting to the flames.

"Unfortunately, they had to leave some expensive equipment behind the brattices, and it's impossible to reach it. So, the boss has decided to dig another entry down from the top of the hill to the mine in order to try to get the equipment from behind the fire."

As the company engineer, Steve had to determine where the entry above the mine would be located in order to come down behind the flames. Though a skilled surveyor, he was concerned about finding the exact spot, no easy task when surveying on top of a steep mountain.

It took several weeks of blasting down through layers and layers of dirt and rocks before the men finally broke through to the area behind the fire. When the new opening came within ten feet of the desired location, Steve was pleased. His boss was happy, too. And I was so proud of my talented husband.

When the hole was large enough, they had to extricate the buried machinery from many feet deep down in the mine. They had to get rescue equipment up to the opening on the hill, but trucks to carry that equipment couldn't handle the nearly vertical slope. So, they used strong mules that hauled it easily up that steep incline. After the abandoned machinery was successfully pulled up from the mine, those sturdy animals hauled all that equipment and the rescued machines back down the hill to be used again. Sometimes, the old ways are better than the new.

After the successful rescue, the company filled in the hole to try to smother the fire. Coal mine fires, with all that available combustible fuel, can burn for years as long as they have any air to feed them. The company assigned men to patrol the hillside above the mine on a regular basis to check for any fissures or openings where smoke was coming out. When they saw any smoke, they would fill those openings with dirt to try to keep a lid on the fire.

Smoke oozes up through the ground from a fire deep in the coal mine below.

Steve thrived on using his engineering skills to solve these and other problems as they arose, both underground and on the surface. When another coal company sued Smith Coal over a boundary dispute, he had to testify in a Louisville court about his surveying findings. The other company lost their suit after he proved that his map of the boundaries was accurate. That got him a nice bonus from the boss.

It gave Steve a great deal of satisfaction to help these mines produce the coal that was so necessary to keep American industry humming. He knew he was doing something useful and helping produce necessary fuel for our country's economy.

I pushed aside my constant fears for his safety, little knowing that tragedy would soon hit close to home.

CHAPTER 19

Tragedy

I knew something was terribly wrong when Steve came home from the mine early, shoulders slumped, head down, his face visibly pale even under the coal dust. I'd never seen him so upset.

"What on earth is the matter?" I asked. "What happened?"

He took a deep breath. "Richard was killed this morning," he said quietly. Richard was the only other engineer employed by the mining company. He was a local man, younger than Steve, with a wife and small child. They lived in a private home near Wooton, and I did not know them.

"Oh, no, Steve! No way! How? What happened?"

"There was a slate fall," Steve explained. "The slate roof of the mine tunnel was unstable, and the heavy rocks broke off, crushing Richard underneath them." He took a deep, unsteady breath, fighting to keep control. "He was working as fire boss and went in before the morning shift to check the quality of air and the safety of the roof. Even though it seemed to be okay when he checked it, it obviously was not."

Steve's voice started trembling, and he paused for a moment to get control before continuing. "He stopped to talk to the buggy driver, who was bringing his buggy into the area they were working, when the roof fell in right on top of him. It smashed his head and killed him instantly. The buggy driver was hurt, but not bad."

"Oh, no! I'm so sorry." I put my arms around him but had no words to express the sick feeling I had inside. Not only was a woman widowed and a child left fatherless, but I knew that it so easily could have been my husband. I hugged him hard, coal dust and all, thankful that he was all right.

Steve pushed on, his voice still a bit shaky. "As the engineer there today, I had to fill out the accident forms before I left the mine. It wasn't easy to write up the death of someone I knew and worked with."

"Oh, Steve. That must have been awful."

Steve nodded. "But it was up to me. It was my responsibility."

We were both shocked and saddened. I'd known all along that the underground coal mining was dangerous, but this tragedy really hammered it home. Richard was young; he had left a young family now bereft. Somehow that made it seem worse.

Our hearts were heavy for Richard's family, but at the same time we faced the realization that Steve might easily have been the one caught under that slate fall. I could have lost him.

"It could have been you," I said, stating the obvious. "Thank God you are all right."

I could tell he was thinking the same thing. "By the grace of God, it wasn't me." He hugged me again and went inside to clean up. It was a sad dinner that night, and neither of us had the heart to talk. Toddy jabbered away, quite oblivious of our distress. He was too young to understand.

They scheduled the funeral for the following Saturday. The rituals of death in Leslie County were far different from any I'd known. Although I expected that all the friends and neighbors would be bringing food and condolences to the family, I was not prepared for the rest of it. The undertaker took Richard's body back to his home, and a visitation was held there the night before the funeral.

"We need to go to the wake," Steve said.

"I'm not comfortable about that, but if it's expected, I guess we must go." I'd never been to a wake, and I didn't know if I could handle it. I tend to cry over sad movies and sad books. How could I keep from crying for a dead man and his family?

"Only for a little while," he said.

"Okay, my love. For your sake and for Richard's family, I will go. But don't expect me to be stoic. I may cry."

"It will be okay if you do," he said, giving me a sweet hug.

I baked a casserole to take to the grieving widow. What an awful word that is: *widow*. It implies such sadness and darkness.

Then I discovered that I didn't have anything black to wear. "Do you suppose it's okay if I wear navy blue?" I asked.

"Of course," Steve said. "Hurry, let's go and get it over with."

When we got to Richard's house, I turned to Steve and said, "What on earth can we say to make things any better?" Though Steve had worked with Richard every day for some months, I'd not known him or his wife well, nor did we know his extended family.

"I really don't know," he said. "Let's just say how sorry we are."

We took our covered dish, said our condolences, and joined the other mourners in the living room. The coffin sat in the middle of the room, supported by two wooden sawhorses. Thankfully, the casket was closed. Chairs were set all around the edges of the room for the mourners.

It was not an uplifting Irish wake, which celebrates the life of the deceased. This was a somber occasion. We sat uncomfortably for what seemed an interminable time, hearing only a few muted comments made by people we didn't know, all the while unable to keep our eyes off the elephant in the middle of the room. The funereal atmosphere quelled much conversation. Richard's widow, eyes red-rimmed and swollen, tried to be hospitable, but she often retreated to her bedroom for some private grieving. It was a sad evening, and we left as soon as we could.

The funeral the next day was another unnerving experience. I'd dreaded it all week. The only funerals I'd attended before were for elderly people; this was for a young man, who had his whole life ahead of him. His small child would never know his father. I had to stop thinking about how I hated this. After all, the funeral was not about me; it was about supporting Richard's family.

As we walked up to the church, Steve said, "I'm going to sing in the choir, remember?"

"Right."

"Hang in there." He squeezed my hand, knowing how upset I was.

Steve joined the choir behind the pulpit, and I found a seat in the back. The church filled up quickly. Richard and his wife had both been born and raised in the county, and they had many relatives and friends there.

The service was long, and many people gave eulogies to extoll Richard's virtues. The choir sang sad hymns, and the preacher gave a fire-and-brimstone sermon, which brought me little comfort. At the end, everyone was herded, in a long line, down to the front of the church to pay their respects to Richard in the casket, now open. My heart sank to my shoes. I didn't really want to see him, knowing that the slate fall had damaged his head and face, but there was no way to avoid the lineup. I averted my eyes, saying a silent prayer for him as I passed by the casket, afraid to look.

It was a relief to get out the door of the church and fill my lungs with fresh air. When Steve caught up with me, he took my hand in his, and we looked at each other, still full of both sorrow and at the same time guilty relief that it hadn't been he who was caught under the slate fall.

The tragedy sobered both of us. After Richard's death, the very real dangers of Steve's working underground were never far from my thoughts. Every morning when I kissed him goodbye, I was always aware that it might be the last time I'd see him alive. The company lost about one man a year in its small mines, which was not really a bad record when compared to the multiple deaths each year in larger mines. However, it was so horrible for the family of that one man.

"Be safe," I'd say.

"I will," he'd answer. "You know I'm careful; don't worry."

Careful or not, one could not always control the unstable conditions of an underground coal mine. Of course, I'd worry.

In spite of the danger, Steve truly loved his job and working underground. He found the work fascinating, and he enjoyed the challenge of using his skills and knowledge to help extract the coal from the ancient beds of those Kentucky mountains. Perhaps he liked the excitement and challenge of the dangers, too. He'd often told me about his dangerous yet exciting experiences in the South Pacific during the four years he served in the Navy during World War II. In spite of the dangers, he truly enjoyed his wartime service. But he would never mention that he found his mining work exciting, knowing of my worries for him.

After the men he worked with got to know him, he enjoyed their camaraderie. Though he was a furriner from outside their world and had a college education to boot, both of which made him suspect, they appreciated his technical knowledge, abilities, and willingness to work hard. They decided he was okay—at least much better than other furriners they knew. And they respected him, calling him "Mistuh Steve."

"Mistuh Steve" shown at the open mouth (adit) of one of the mines where he worked.

I tried to put aside my worries about his safety, knowing he was happy with his work. When I saw his car drive up after work, though, I would immediately feel a sense of peace, which lasted only until the next morning when he went off to the mines again. I never lost that nagging sense of unease until we came back West where he had safer working conditions in potash and copper mines.

I learned a hard lesson from Richard's tragic death. I came to realize how precious each day is and to truly understand that we never know what might happen tomorrow. I began to try to appreciate each day for the blessings it brought, rather than always looking back and longing for what was or looking ahead and wishing for what will be. I tried to adopt as my mantra the verse from the Bible that says, "This is the day the Lord hath made; let us rejoice and be glad in it." I did, and I still do, "rejoice and be glad in it."

I think I was beginning to grow up.

CHAPTER 20

A Best Friend

A red convertible with its top down was parked in the street below my kitchen window. Sitting at the wheel was an attractive young woman with a little girl about Toddy's age standing in the seat beside her. Dressed fashionably, lovely hairstyle, and driving a fancy car, the woman didn't look like any of the local mountain people. The car alone shrieked cool and trendy like an automobile ad from a magazine. I wondered who she was and wished I had the nerve to go down and talk to her. She was about my age. Could she become a friend, perhaps?

I really missed having someone my own age to talk to. Our neighbors were such good people and filled my need for conversation with other adults, but most of our discussions seemed to cover only cooking or housekeeping or the weather or children. As wonderful as Mrs. McGee was to me, she was more like my mom than a contemporary. Even her daughter, Kathleen, was ten years older than I. Besides, she worked hard every day and had little time to visit when she came home.

The veterans-housing project where we had lived the previous year in Colorado had been filled with young families. I could always find someone who had read the same book as I had or who knew how to deal with the baby's teething or colic or where to go to find a bargain in a local store. My classes at the university had been stimulating and interesting, and I missed having conversations and discussions about current events, books, and politics.

Most of all, I missed having a best friend, having left behind in Denver a wonderful soul mate who has been a lifelong friend. I wrote frequent letters to family and friends, subscribed to many magazines, and read the newspaper from cover to cover, but I still needed someone with whom to discuss more than cooking or child care, someone who was interested in what was going on in the country, who knew more of the world than just the hill country of Appalachia. Though Steve was often willing to talk about these things, I was hungry for female companionship.

One day when I was shopping in the company store, I was delighted to see the young woman from the convertible there with her little curly-headed daughter. When the little girl spotted Toddy, she ran over to talk to him, as children often do.

"Hi, I'm Linda," the cute little blonde said to Toddy. That impulsive gesture on her part provided the magic for our meeting.

When her mom joined us, I gathered up my courage and said, "Hi. This is Toddy and I'm Margie. We live upstairs."

"And I'm Sally," Linda's mom said with a smile. "I live in Wooton."

She already knew who I was, thanks to the small community grapevine, and we struck up a conversation. That was the beginning of a wonderful friendship that we would share for the rest of the time we lived in Kentucky.

A city girl who grew up in in Lexington, Kentucky, Sally had been a furriner too. She'd arrived in Leslie County to work as a secretary for Mary Breckinridge, the founder of the Frontier Nursing Service. The FNS provided modern nursing and midwifery service to mothers and their babies in the hills and hollers of the county.

While working for Mrs. Breckinridge, Sally had met her husband, Paul. His family owned and ran the small country store in nearby Wooton, the nearest little community to our coal camp. Because his parents had a secure income, they had been able to send Paul out of the hills to boarding school in Berea, south of Lexington, where he received a good education. He would tell us about the daylong trip by muleback over the mountains (before the roads were cut through) to get to Hazard, where he could catch a train to Berea.

Service in the army during World War II further broadened Paul's horizons, and he and Sally found they had much in common. They'd fallen in love and married, and they now lived near his family in Wooton with their small daughter, Linda. Paul owned and operated some of the trucks that transported coal from the mines to the tipple at the railhead in Hazard.

Sally and I soon became fast friends. Our children played well together, and we spent many happy hours discussing what we thought were important issues—clothes and books and politics and local issues—while our children were playing. It was so good to have someone to talk to who was about my age, and we consumed many cups of coffee as we got acquainted and shared ideas. I had finally learned to drink coffee when I had to get up at five o'clock to make Steve breakfast and pack his lunch to take to work. But it always tasted better when I shared it with Sally as we sat at her kitchen table or mine.

Best friends Linda Muncy and Toddy Conder playing together.

Sally had attended a two-year college for women, as had I before I transferred to a four-year university, and that provided one link immediately as we compared notes on our experiences in a women's college. Since she had been living in the area for some years, I was eager to learn how she had adapted to the hill customs. She explained and interpreted a great many mysteries for me, and with increased understanding of local customs, I became less of a furriner. I don't think I could have gotten through those four years in Kentucky without her and her sage advice.

Soon, we began to get together with our husbands. Not too many social activities livened up the coal camp, but we made our own fun. We went on many picnics together, driving to an unpopulated area by some crick, where we could spread out our meal and watch our little ones splash in the water. Sally and I chatted while our husbands washed their cars and Paul fished. We often enjoyed fish fries as well, relishing the succulent fish that Paul caught. We celebrated holidays together and shared many meals. It was a wonderful and rewarding friendship.

That friendship expanded to Paul's family. His sister, Helen, who lived near them in Wooton, once entertained us for dinner. A marvelous cook, she served us a delicious meal, but she did not sit down with us to eat. Typical of the traditional mountain custom, I was to learn, she waited on us hand and foot to make sure that we enjoyed her hospitality, while her husband, Paul and Sally, and Steve and I sat at the table and scarfed down all her mouthwatering southern cooking.

It made me uncomfortable to have her wait on us, but she would not let us help. It was as if she felt fully responsible for making sure that we enjoyed every minute of our evening. All my upbringing told me this was not right; a wife is not just a servant. I think my suffragette grandmother's genes were talking to me. However, one does not challenge the customs of a hostess, and reluctantly, I had the good sense to relax and enjoy our meal.

That night, I gained a new insight into the role of women in the mountains of Appalachia at that time. The emancipation of women that had occurred in most of the United States during the first half of the twentieth century had not yet penetrated these isolated communities of eastern Kentucky in the 1950s. Still living as their grandparents and great-grandparents had for several centuries, the local people expected their women to take care of their homes and children and be subservient to their husbands. Working outside the home was practically unheard of for the women of the area. I knew of only two married women employed at that time: Kathleen, who worked in the company store, and her sister, who worked in an office in town.

Though I was not a subservient wife (just ask Steve!), I did enjoy being a stay-at-home mom. Looking back at the mid-twentieth century, I can't help but think that we women who were able to be home with our small children were very fortunate. Though we didn't have the incomes that working couples have today, we had the time to enjoy each hour of each day with our babies and toddlers and adolescents as they grew up. We had the time to practice those economies that made it possible to get by on one income. We didn't eat out; I sewed clothing for the children and myself; we seldom went out to movies or other entertainment; I shopped carefully. We didn't have expensive computers, cell phones, media equipment; they weren't even invented then. Later, when faced with college bills for three children, I would start my teaching career, but I still treasure the memories of those years I had at home with my children.

Sally introduced us to a small Episcopal church in Wooton, up the hill from the store. Steve and I were both Episcopalians; we had been married in Saint Stephen's church in my Arizona hometown. I was surprised but delighted to learn about the little mission church hidden in the hills. The priest in Hazard and his wife drove to Wooton for occasional services, and we enjoyed their friendship. Though we did not attend very regularly, we did enjoy the rustic beauty of the church and the delightful people who attended services there. Toddy and his baby brother, Michael, were both baptized there. The church was probably the legacy of those British men and women who settled in eastern Kentucky two hundred years earlier. Attending that church was the start of many years of fulfilling and rewarding relationship with the Episcopal Church.

For the most part, the local people were people of faith. Their religion was a very important part of their lives. Most of them attended the Baptist church, but we also knew of a fundamentalist offshoot church nearby, where the members practiced snake handling to prove their faith in God. Though most of those who were bitten survived, we learned that a child had died nearby from the deadly venom of a rattlesnake. In those days, no antivenin was available, at least not in our rural area. I had a hard time reconciling my belief in a mother's responsibility to care for her child with the practice of exposing that child to a such a deadly threat.

A year or two after we met Sally and Paul, he decided to build a drive-in movie theater. An entrepreneur at heart, Paul enjoyed having and running his own businesses. A movie theater was a big deal for Wooton, a tiny community set in a clearing by the road containing his family's small general store and post office, plus a few homes and the church in the hills nearby. A drive-in theater would be a marvelous new source of entertainment for the residents of this isolated area.

One day, Paul called Steve for help. "I need to build a sign to advertise the drive-in," he said. "I want to locate it by the road, where people can see it, because the drive-in itself is hidden up on the hill behind the store."

"What do you need?" Steve asked him.

"Some design help. I know how to build it, but I'm not sure what I want it to look like and the specifics for the construction.

"Sure thing, Paul. I'll draw up some plans for you to look at after I do some measuring."

Steve, with his engineering and drafting background, drew the plans for the marquee. We had fun watching the construction of the project, checking on it frequently. It turned out well, looking very professional. Before long, it was time for the opening night.

The movie marquee that Steve Conder designed displays the movie showing that week at the new Wooton drive-in movie theater.

The first movie they showed was a western shoot-'em-up, which Paul knew would appeal to the hill people.

"I can't wait to see a movie again," I said. We hadn't been to one since we'd left Denver.

"When is opening night?" Steve asked.

"Next Saturday. We can put Toddy in the back seat to sleep."

"Sounds good. It should be fun."

When we arrived just about dusk, with Toddy in his pajamas, a huge crowd had gotten there ahead of us. The grand opening was not to be missed! To our surprise, there were as many or more wagons and mules as there were cars. Everyone had come down from the hills and hollers for the big event. The families in the wagons were a wonderful sight to see. They had put kitchen chairs in the wagon beds for seats for the whole family to watch the movie, and everybody was all dressed up in their Sunday best. Even the mules that pulled the wagons were dressed for the occasion, sporting tinkling bells and colorful tassels on their shiny, polished harnesses. It was a momentous event for these country folks, many of whom had never seen a movie.

Mules pulling the wagons display tinkling bells, tassels and polished harnesses at the momentous first showing of a movie in the new drive-in. More patrons came in wagons than in cars.

The movie was a great success, and we spent many a Saturday night after that watching old westerns from our car, complete with homemade popcorn and our son asleep in the back seat.

Our friendship with Sally and Paul and their family remains one of the highlights of our years in the hill country. We had much in common, and they filled our need for friends our own age. We'll always be grateful for their loving, caring relationship, which enriched our lives in so many ways.

CHAPTER 21

Gastronomic Goodies

"Mrs. McGee, what are you cooking? It smells really good," I called as I stuck my head into her apartment door one day not long after we had moved into the apartment.

"Why it's jist plain old pinto beans," she replied as she came to the door.

"Really? The smell makes my mouth water. Would you tell me how you cook them please?"

"Shore 'nuf." She smiled. "It's easy as pie. Jist warsh them and pick out the stones and put 'em in a big pot of water to soak all night. Next day, throw in a slab of salt pork and cook 'em for all day until they're soft. That's all there is to it."

Hmmm. Doesn't sound too hard.

So, I tried my luck with a pot of beans made from scratch. "Shore 'nuf," they were "right good."

Steve asked, "Could I have seconds?"

"Of course," I replied. "I'm so glad you like them."

That's when I knew I had scored. They were so much better than a can of beans.

"But next time, how about you fix corn bread with them?" My husband had grown up in Tennessee and knew all about southern (or "southren," as he called it) cooking.

"Of course, my darling. As soon as I learn to make it."

One of my great joys of our four-year sojourn in Kentucky was learning to cook the delicious southern food that we so enjoyed eating. I picked the brains of all my neighbors and friends to find out what they were cooking and how they cooked it.

The simple and inexpensive dish of pinto beans was a staple for the local people, providing much-needed protein for the poorer families who might not have the money to buy meat very often. Though I might have served them with tortillas in Arizona, here in the mountains of Kentucky, they were served with corn bread to make a complete meal.

Mrs. McGee and Kathleen taught me a great deal about Kentucky cooking. After two years of marriage, I knew enough to feed us adequately, but I had so much more to learn. I'd prepared mostly basic meals during those two years when we were both in college and had very little money. Lots of hamburgers, chili con carne, spaghetti, Mexican food and anything I could make from ground beef or chicken, which were not too expensive.

However, this southern cooking was an entirely different proposition, and I was hooked early on. Every meal we'd eaten at the Hyden boardinghouse—and every meal we ate in someone else's home—introduced me to new gastronomic delights. I was determined to learn to prepare some of them myself.

Next on my list was the corn bread Steve had asked for, and I pinned down my next-door neighbor.

"Kathleen, would you show me how you fix that yummy corn bread you make?"

"You bet. Do you want to come over this evenin' and watch me make it for our supper?"

"I'll be there." Thank goodness I now knew what time evenin' was.

When I knocked on her door, Kathleen led me into her kitchen. She already had the oven on and was assembling the ingredients on the table: eggs, white cornmeal, baking powder, salt, and milk. She popped her black iron skillet in the oven to melt a chunk of lard. While it was heating, she beat the eggs in a bowl, blended in the dry ingredients, and poured enough milk in the bowl to make a juicy batter. She pulled out the skillet and poured the batter on top of the melted lard in the skillet.

"That's all there is to it," Kathleen said, smiling at me.

"How long do you bake it?"

"Oh, about twenty minutes or so, until it's done."

"Okay. Thanks so much. That doesn't look too hard. I'll go home and try it."

"Oh, stay and have a piece," she said.

I did, and it melted in my mouth.

However, the first time I tried to bake southern corn bread myself, it was a dismal flop. Kathleen hadn't measured anything she put in her batter, but I thought I knew about how much of each ingredient she used. Not so. Either too much of one thing or not enough of the other. And I had to buy lard because I had always used shortening for baking. Completely different flavor. I persisted, though, and finally got my corn bread to taste good enough to serve with a smile.

That night at dinner, Steve said, "Hey, Margie. This corn bread is pretty good." High praise from the man of the house. He always enjoyed his food, but he didn't always vocalize his appreciation.

"Thank you. I worked at it!"

"Well, I hope you make it again because I really like it."

My corn bread never tasted quite as good as Kathleen's, but it went very well with pinto beans and also with fried fish.

We were lucky enough to enjoy many fish fries while we lived in the backwoods. Fish were plentiful in the creeks and branches, and the local fishermen often shared some of their catches. After eating some luscious, crisp-fried fish, I knew I had to learn how to cook it. In another life, I had learned to cook fish the way my mom did. She had just floured the fish and cooked them over a medium heat.

I went back to Mrs. McGee and said, "Would you show me how

107

you fry fish? It's just so good the way you do it." I felt a bit disloyal to my mom, but crisp was so much better.

"Why, shore 'nuf. I'm a-fixin' it this evenin'. Come on over before supper."

When I got there, she was already preparing the fish, which her husband had caught and then cleaned for her.

"You need yer big arn skillet to start," she said. "Jest pour in a goodly bit of lard an' het it up." Those iron skillets are versatile cooking implements. Bake your corn bread, fry your fish, whatever.

"Meantimes, you dip yer fish in egg what's beaten up, then in flour, then in cornmeal. Be shore that skillet is toasty hot an' fry it up right quick on one side and then t'other."

Well, that was the best fish I ever ate. I never fried it again the way my mom did after I first tasted that crisp, cornmeal coating. And now I could serve it with corn bread.

Crisp-fried chicken needs the same high heat, I learned. Again, frying as my mother had taught me was to brown it and then lower the heat and cover it until done. Southern style, one must keep the heat high and cook it fast and uncovered so it gets crisp. Yums. Now when I fry chicken, that's the way I do it. My cuisine skills were changing, and for the better, I thought, though I felt a bit disloyal to my mom.

Mrs. McGee taught me to cook many main dishes as well as southern style vegetables. My favorites included her not only fried chicken and fish but also barbecue pork and country-smoked ham. Of course, all were full of unhealthy fat, especially if they were fried in lard or bacon grease, but they were oh, so good! In those days, we knew nothing about the dangers of high cholesterol, and we enjoyed every bit of those fried foods.

Southern-style barbecue pork is mouthwatering good. It is cooked slowly for a long time over low heat and then shredded, and the barbecue sauce is added afterward. The western barbecue I had always known was made with beef. Because we lived in ranching country in Arizona, it was natural to use beef, which was plentiful and not too expensive. It is very good, but it didn't compare to the barbecue pork we ate in Kentucky.

The first time I ate country-smoked ham, I could not believe it was the same meat we'd called ham! It was sweet and succulent and tinged with the delicious flavor from being cured over a smoky fire in someone's barn. It was not always available, but when I found it I snatched it up.

Fresh vegetables in the hill country were quite different from those I'd grown up with. Most of the local people had their own vegetable gardens, and I was introduced to many new varieties of fresh vegetables. Steve, having grown up in the South, was familiar with most of them.

Okra was one that I'd never eaten before, and I had to learn to like it. This slimy vegetable, cooked with tomatoes and onions, was not something I really enjoyed, but when I ate it fried with a cornmeal coating, it became another wonderful regular in our diet. I don't remember who taught me to dip the sliced okra in beaten egg and then in cornmeal and fried (again!). The slime was gone, and the result was simply delicious. I still prepare it this way.

Greens of all kinds—from spinach to mustard and turnip greens—came accompanied with vinegar in a small glass cruet. I learned to cook them but did not eat them with much gusto. Steve, however, enjoyed them all. His mother had prepared greens often when he was growing up. They always had to be served with vinegar. Every kitchen table I saw in Kentucky had a cruet of vinegar beside the salt and pepper.

Black-eyed peas were another dish new to me.

"Look, Steve. I cooked black-eyed peas tonight."

"Wow, what a treat! I haven't had these in a very long time. What's the occasion?"

"Well, a neighbor gave me a batch from her garden, and I wanted to try cooking them. I added some salt pork to the pot."

"These are really good," he said.

I grinned. It's always nice to get a compliment.

"Wouldn't they be good with some hot sauce?" he asked. He has always loved spicy foods. Now he has combined southern-style black-eyed peas with a western touch, adding jalapeño peppers. I'm don't know that the local Kentuckians would approve, though they did use spicy hot sauce with some dishes.

Cucumbers fresh from a friend's garden turned out to be a surprising treat for me. They were one vegetable I had never much liked. The flavor didn't appeal to me, and I could never understand why anyone would eat a silly little cucumber sandwich or even put it in a salad. But once I ate southern-style cucumbers with onions and vinegar at the boardinghouse, I had to learn how to make them myself.

"Mrs. Combs," I asked, "will you show me how you fixed those cucumbers?"

"Yes, ma'am," she said. "Jist come down to my kitchen, and I'll show you. It's right easy to do."

I watched as she sliced the cucumbers crosswise and an onion into rings. "After you cut these 'uns up, you pour over some vinegar and a spoonful of sugah and a bit of water. Then put 'em in the fridge and soak 'em a while."

The result had me convinced that cucumbers are indeed very edible—even delicious. I still fix them many years later.

We enjoyed all the other fresh garden vegetables the local people raised in the summertime and shared freely with us. Fresh corn on the cob, vine-ripened tomatoes, and green beans picked fresh all tasted so much better than anything I could buy in the supermarket.

When we first arrived, I knew nothing about southern-style green beans. One afternoon, I walked into Mrs. McGee's kitchen and saw a big uncovered pot bubbling away on her stove. It was hours before mealtime, and I couldn't figure out what she would be cooking at that time of day. It didn't smell like pinto beans.

"Mrs. McGee?" I called.

"Come on in, Margie," she called back.

"What are you cooking?" I asked as she appeared in the kitchen door.

"Jist green beans."

"Do you cook them for a really long time?"

"Yep, they need to git tender and tasty."

"So, how do you fix them?"

"Oh, I jest string 'em and break 'em up and put them in a big pot of water along with a slab of salt pork."

"Is that all?" I asked.

"Yep. Here, have a bite." She fished out a spoonful of the beans for me to try.

"Well, they sure have a good flavor," I said after swallowing a bite. I found them coated with the fat and a lot of flavor from the salt pork. Not bad, nice flavor indeed. Hmm. A bit greasy. A lot greasy, but I did appreciate the flavor. And were they tender!

When I tried fixing green beans the way Mrs. McGee had, Steve said, "These are really good—so much better than you usually make them. Very tasty."

I beamed. They weren't my favorite with all the grease, but since Steve liked them, I cooked them that way. If a dish had fat in it, he enjoyed it. No wonder he ended up taking cholesterol medicine later in life! He really enjoyed well-done vegetables, which was how his mother had cooked them. I still prefer my green beans a bit crisper—and a bit less greasy. I can't bring myself to cook them with more than a bit of salt pork, enough to flavor but not to coat every bite. Greasy beans? No way.

Now that I had conquered corn bread (sort of), biscuits became one more bread item that I wanted to learn how to make. My friend Sally made the best ones; most of my other cooking mentors served corn bread with their everyday meals. Sally's light and fluffy biscuits were mouthwatering, and I begged her to show me how to make them.

"Come on over, and we'll bake a batch together," Sally suggested.

"Sounds great," I said. I packed Toddy in the car, and off we went.

Sally showed me the ingredients first: flour, baking powder, baking soda, shortening—not having grown up in the hill country, she didn't use lard—salt, and buttermilk. She incorporated the dry ingredients into the shortening, slowly, and then added a small amount of buttermilk. When the dough held together, she stopped to illustrate her directions.

"Now comes the tricky part," she said.

She formed the batter into a ball, placed it on a floured tabletop, and began to knead it gently. "Why don't you try it? You can't do this fast and hard—or you will ruin the biscuits!"

The dough felt spongy and light under my hands as I kneaded. It was lovely to feel.

"That's enough," Sally said. "Next, we will roll out the dough with a rolling pin." Her expert hands quickly had the dough configured in a rough circle about half an inch thick. "Not too thick," she said. "And don't handle it any more than you have it, so it doesn't get tough." When she finished, she said, "Now, would you like to cut it into rounds?"

"Oh, yes, I would."

She gave me an old frozen orange juice can, a small one, with the bottom cut out as well as the top. I carefully cut rounds into the dough, and placed each one, with the sides touching, in a round, greased cake pan.

"We'll bake them at 425 degrees for about fifteen to twenty minutes," Sally said.

I could smell them within five minutes, and my mouth started watering. When they were done, they were a lovely, light brown, high in the pan. Beautiful.

"After they cool," Sally said, "you take half of them for you and Steve to have with your dinner tonight.

"You don't have to persuade me," I said.

Steve loved them, and I made several batches until I finally was happy with my own biscuits. I learned the hard way to use that very light hand in kneading and rolling out the dough. The final products were not as good as Sally's, perhaps, but they were still pretty tasty.

Baking desserts was another learning experience. Neither of us could resist scarfing down whatever sweet treats came our way during those years we lived in the Kentucky backwoods. Southern desserts were always mouthwatering delights: everything from homemade pies to towering layer cakes to delicate custards to scrumptious cobblers.

My favorite? Chess pie. I'd never heard of chess pie before. What a strange name. And stranger still were the ingredients. It is made with vinegar and cornmeal! It is a rich and sweet and delicious pie. Addictive, even. I found it hard to stop with one piece, even though its name sounded strange to this westerner. I think, though, that chess pie has spread out West since I see recipes for it in magazines now. Of course, peach pie made from fresh peaches was my second favorite. Yums.

Sally also persuaded me to bake angel food cakes from scratch. I'd never have even tried them if it were not for her. Using a dozen eggs?

What if I messed up in dividing the yolks and got a bit of yellow in with the whites? The whole batch would be ruined! Well, the answer was simple. Divide them one at a time over two bowls. Then add each white to the big bowl before separating the next one. What to do with all those yolks? Why make a yellow cake, of course. Steve was in hog heaven to have two cakes to choose from.

Hill country cuisine was so very different from what I had known growing up in the West, but I had great joy in learning new ways of cooking and new items to cook. I began to feel as if I were fitting in with those southern neighbors. And we were enjoying much better meals than I had ever cooked before. I still enjoy preparing many of those southern dishes, and I send up thanks to all those wonderful Kentucky women who taught me how to fix them.

CHAPTER 22

Counting Our Blessings

"Good news, Margie!" Steve almost bounced into the apartment.

"What? What's going on?"

"You'll never guess!"

"Tell me then. Tell me!" I laughed.

"We're getting the house!"

"Really? I can't believe it. That's wonderful! I've been hoping we'd get it, but hoping doesn't make it so."

We'd watched the empty house on the corner below our apartment for several months, wishing it were ours to rent. Now it would be.

*The brick home with a porch swing and the picket fence built by
the author's husband, where they lived from 1952-1955.*

We were delighted. No more climbing those steep stairs, and we
would have a yard for our two-year-old son to play in. It sounded like
heaven to us. For the first time in our marriage, we would have a real
house instead of an apartment, a place we could plant a flower garden
and enjoy sitting on the front porch swing. Toddy could run around in
the yard, ride his tricycle, and dig in the dirt as little boys love to do.

The traditional red brick house sat six or eight steps aboveground
with a small basement for a coal furnace underneath. It had a nice-sized
living room, a separate dining room, a large kitchen, three bedrooms
and a bath, and covered front and back porches. Heaven!

We packed up our things and hired the strong McGee boys to move
our furniture down to the house. Our move down was a whole lot easier
than the move upstairs had been, even though we had considerably
more to move than we'd had a year and a half earlier. It was lovely to
be able to place it all into rooms of the house, which immediately felt
like home.

Though smaller in square feet than the apartment, it had a separate
dining room and felt larger and certainly more convenient than having
all the rooms open off one side of the long hall. With the living room just
inside the front door, we enjoyed sitting there every day. The apartment

living room at the end of the long hall was seldom used unless we had company. As we unpacked everything, I rejoiced in having a house with a yard. What a happy day!

One of the first things Steve did was to build a white picket fence around the yard to provide Toddy a safe place to play outside. Because the company store was directly across the side street, we had much traffic coming and going right beside the house, including huge coal trucks. I still cherish the memory of Toddy "helping" his daddy with that fence.

From the front porch swing, we could see across the highway, down Cutshin Creek and to the wooded hills beyond. We spent many a happy hour on that swing. We enjoyed planting bushes and flowers in our backyard and flowers in the planter box on the front porch. Each new bloom brought me more joy.

The porch swing brings many happy moments for the Conder family. Here the author holds baby Michael while son Toddy grins at his mom.

The Franks lived next door, closer to the creek, and Grace gave me starters of many perennial flowers. The couple proved to be wonderful neighbors, good Christian folk with all that word implies: kindness, thoughtfulness, loving, and caring. We had lucked out again.

We soon bought a few more pieces of furniture, which helped fill up the empty third bedroom that Steve used as an office, but the best purchase of all was my automatic washing machine. We had bought the old, used wringer washer in Denver when Toddy was born, and I'd used it ever since. Though better than washing clothes by hand, it still involved a good deal of work and time. I was happy to get rid of it, and I loved my automatic washer. Put in the clothes and soap, punch the start button, and leave. Now I really enjoyed doing the laundry each week. We often had mountains of dirty clothing; with the ever-present coal dust and the unpaved street beside our home, I had a constant battle to fight. Toddy loved to play in the black dirt.

I did feel a bit guilty when I watched the coal camp women who had to heat their wash water over an open fire and haul it bucket by bucket up the porch to their wringer washers. I counted my blessings for my automatic spin-dry washer and real clothesline in the backyard. In the apartment, I had to hang my laundry on the furniture or a rack. The clothes smelled so clean and fresh after bringing them in from the line.

Our fortunes were improving, and life was good. As Steve got some nice raises, we traded in our trusty old '39 Chevrolet and bought a new car. Brand-new. It was a small, two-door coupé, but it seemed like the most wonderful car in the world. After dealing with the mechanical problems of old cars ever since we were married, it was great to have reliable transportation. It even allowed us to drive to Florida to visit Steve's folks for a real vacation a year or two later.

It seemed as though "our cup runneth over" that fall of 1952. The joy of our new home and newfound friends was compounded by the beauty of autumn in the mountains of Kentucky. The early frosts painted rainbows of glorious colors on the mountainsides. Interspersed among the dark evergreens, the dazzling array of fall colors—scarlets, golds, oranges, and bronzes—took my breath away. I reveled in those vivid hues of maples and oaks and black walnuts and other hardwood trees as their leaves changed. The brilliant tapestry was a glorious sight.

Someone once said that we surrender to power unwillingly; to beauty willingly. I certainly surrendered completely to the beauty of those mountains. I was content and happy with my new life in Kentucky.

It's no wonder that my nesting instinct took over at that time. Toddy was two and a half by then, and we began thinking about adding to our family now that we had a real house of our own and more income. I was thrilled when I found I was pregnant in the fall of 1952. Could life be any better?

Sadly, this baby was not to be. I suffered a miscarriage early on in my pregnancy, and I was devastated. As the days grew shorter that fall and winter, I grew sad and depressed. The joy of the new house and the new car was gone. The gorgeous fall colors of the hardwood trees faded, and every day we woke up to gray skies, rain, and damp cold that crept into our bones.

When the incessant winter rains started, I felt as though the heavens were weeping along with me. Born and raised in sunny, dry Arizona, I remember thinking that I would give all my fortune to be able to see the sun again. I grew homesick with my family so far away, and I mourned the loss of our unborn baby. I wallowed in a great deal of self-pity, which was not improved by the gloomy weather.

We had a very wet winter that year, days and days of rain coming down in solid sheets. Cutshin Creek, only about fifty feet from our house, rose quickly as it absorbed those heavy rains. We watched the muddy water, brown as boiling gravy, rise rapidly, a foot or so a day. I'd not thought much about the yearly floods when we were living in the second-floor apartment, but now it was very close to us.

I became really concerned when I began to see large items bobbing down the raging water. Pieces of wood, a roll of barbed wire, fence posts, a chicken coop, and even an outhouse rode down the creek, dislodged from upriver by the raging water. One day, I looked out and saw a whole house floating down the middle of the swollen river that the creek had become. It wobbled and turned, and then it slammed against the bridge. The house was too big and the water too high for it to go underneath, so it battered itself against the bridge, disintegrating slowly, piece by piece. It broke my heart to think of the family who had lived in it.

House carried down swollen Cutshin Creek smashes against the bridge and ends up in many pieces on the flooded road

Clyde and Grace's home, next door to ours, was on the creek's edge and lower than ours, so we were all concerned that the floodwater would rise high enough to get into their house. Every day, we watched the creek grow bigger and bigger, a foot or two at a time, relentlessly devouring all the land at its edges. We really worried when the water licked at the foundation of their house. It looked like the flood would never stop growing.

Finally, the water began to recede—but not until after Clyde and Grace's whole yard had become a large wading pool. I breathed a sigh of relief for them—and for us as well. A foot or two higher, and it would have been in our yard and our basement, ruining the furnace and everything stored there. Sadly, the spring floods were a yearly occurrence, and we learned to expect the high water to arrive every year after the heavy winter rains.

The arrival of spring finally broke my bout of depression. Springtime in the hill country rivaled the beauty of autumn, with bright and cheerful light, a promise of good weather to come after the dismal winter.

The vivid hot pinks of blossoming redbud trees and the creamy white flowers of dogwood trees painted colorful polka dots among the evergreen pines on the hillsides. I'd never seen these flowering trees in the West, and I was entranced. Wildflowers splashed cheerful colors all over the hills and hollers. Bright-yellow daffodils and white crocuses grew wild too, rampant everywhere one could see, under the trees, alongside the road. Wild irises, called *flags* in that part of the country, raised their lavender and purple blossoms to the sunshine.

White dogwood blossoms gladden the Kentucky hills in springtime, blooming by a split rail fence.

I often sat on the porch swing and breathed in the scents of new growth, flowers, and sunshine, admiring the spectacular view up the hillsides. Best of all, I was pregnant again. Our second son—although we did not know it was a boy ahead of time—was due in November 1953, and his impending arrival brightened my spirits as much as the return of spring did. I felt exhilarated even as I dealt with the challenges of morning sickness. Life was good again for us in the hills of Kentucky.

This pregnancy was uneventful, thank goodness, and each day that passed eased my fear of another miscarriage. My doctor's office was in Hazard, twenty-five miles and forty-five minutes away on good days. It was always a breathtaking trip over the narrow, winding roads. The maniacs who drove the big trucks that hauled coal from the mines to the tipple in Hazard thought they owned the road. One had to expect to meet a truck on the wrong side of the road around every curve. I always felt relieved when we arrived in Hazard safely.

I liked my small-town doctor. He always treated me with respect and caring, and we shared many a philosophical discussion after discussing the progress of my pregnancy. One day when I showed up for my appointment, he was shaking his head in dismay. His previous patient had brought in her baby to be treated for a sore throat with a string tied around his neck.

"What's that string doing there?" he asked the baby's mother.

"Why, that's jist to cure his sore throat," she said.

"Well, it didn't cure it, did it? Let's try some of my medicine. I think that will do a better job."

Of course, he prescribed an antibiotic, a bit more effective than string in curing what may have been strep throat. Maybe that mom learned that modern medicine is sometimes better than folk medicine.

He groaned a bit as he told me the story. The superstitious hill people still used folk medicine and advice handed down to them from many generations back to treat their illnesses. With no doctors available in that mountainous area for many years, they relied solely on local herbs (*yarbs*), and superstitions for medical treatment. Though many herbs and poultices can be effective in treating illnesses, they cannot do what modern medicine can.

When it was time for our baby to be born, we hired a local woman to take care of three-year-old Toddy while I was in the hospital in Hazard. She was very nervous about working for us furriners, with our strange ways, but she gamely took on the job. I'm surprised she didn't have a nervous breakdown when we left in such a rush that I had no time to tell her what I was cooking. I had started the meat sauce for spaghetti, which was not a familiar dish for her, and I decided I better not take the time to finish it. I have no idea what she did with it, and I didn't ask.

It was a harrowing trip across the mountain's dangerous roads that November day. We were dodging the coal trucks—the labor pains were coming faster and faster—and Steve was driving faster and faster. We arrived in Hazard in the nick of time. Michael William was born about thirty minutes later, a joyful addition to our family.

After the baby and I spent four or five days in the hospital, the usual time for new mothers to stay in those days, we brought our new little son home. Our sitter had managed to struggle through, and Steve and Toddy seemed to have survived my absence.

Michael was an adorable baby. He was generally happy and agreeable, and there was no trace of the colic that Toddy had during his first few months. We adored him, of course, and so did Toddy. Michael was a loving child, who warmed our hearts. It was only later that we discovered his mischievous side. It started the day he managed to throw his strained beets from his highchair onto the ceiling—only the first of many pranks. I never did get the red stain completely off the ceiling.

Baby Michael dumps out his breakfast onto his highchair, not on the ceiling this time.

We loved having our second little boy. Our family felt full and complete (though we were delighted a few years later to add a much-wanted little girl). It was a busy time for me with two little ones to care for, but I enjoyed being a mom almost every minute—except when Michael woke me up before dawn every day, cheerful and wide awake, wanting to get up right now!

Toddy was fascinated by his baby brother, and he couldn't keep his hands off this new, delightful little creature. He enjoyed holding him, under supervision, of course, and thought the new baby was created for his own amusement. Finally, we bought him a small doll stroller and a little boy doll so that he could have his own baby boy to take care of when Mom had to take care of the real baby. He enjoyed that stroller for quite a while; it soon became a car or a truck or a fire engine or any other vehicle he could think of. Anything on wheels was a great toy. The novelty of the new baby faded, the doll went by the wayside, and he went back to his little boy's toys.

I felt fulfilled and joyous again after the winter of depression the year before. When the skies grew dark and dreary with winter rain, I now had my expanded family to enjoy. The chores of motherhood and housekeeping filled my days, but we also had a new source of entertainment.

Before Michael was born, the coal company had put up an antenna tower on the hill above the hollow so that the coal camp could receive television programming. This momentous development would change the lives of many of the local people. It introduced a whole new world to them, and they began to learn about what was going on in our country and elsewhere in the world. It was a real revelation to those mountain people who had never ventured far from home.

Our next-door neighbors bought the first television in the coal camp.

"Come over and watch with us," Grace said. When we did, we were awestruck to see this marvelous new machine that had pictures and sound.

"And have Toddy come over to watch a children's show in the morning," Grace said.

"Oh, he will like that," I replied.

I loved watching our three-year-old trudge down the driveway all by himself and over to her house every morning to see "Romper Room." He was very proud of going off by himself. We finally bought our own TV set shortly before Michael's birth.

In 1953, TV was still pretty primitive, black-and-white only, no remote control, but we thought it was wonderful. It brought the outside world to us in our small little holler. I was delighted. I'd been subscribing to half a dozen magazines in order to learn what was happening in the outside world, including a weekly news magazine, but this wonderful invention brought instant news and entertaining shows. Suddenly the world was at our fingertips, and this isolated area was isolated no more from the rest of the world.

We'd not had the TV very long when, early in December, a few weeks after we brought Michael home, we had a monstrous snow and ice storm. Huge icicles hung from the power lines, which went down under the weight, and we suddenly found ourselves in dire straits with no electricity.

We had no lights, water, or heat. Our coal furnace had a thermostat and an automatic stoker that didn't work without electricity. We had no fireplace to heat the house, and it cooled off very fast in the frigid temperature. The water for the coal camp was pumped from a well with an electric motor. My cookstove was electric; I couldn't cook or make formula for the baby. We were completely dependent on electricity, and we had none with the lines down.

When Steve came home that day, the house was already icy. I bundled up the little boys and myself, but it was cold. Fortunately, I'd already made Michael's formula, but I couldn't warm it up. We couldn't stay in the house, but we also couldn't get out of the coal camp because snow and ice made the mountain roads impassable. With a brand-new baby and a three-year-old, I was frantic.

"Steve, what on earth are we going to do?"

"Maybe I can borrow a camp stove from a friend."

"That might allow us to melt some snow for water and formula, but it won't warm up the house."

Fortunately, about that time, Grace called. "We want you to move in with us. I know you don't have heat, and you can't stay there with a new baby." They had heat because their hand-stoked coal furnace was not dependent upon an electric thermostat.

"Thank you, thank you! You are a lifesaver, literally, Grace. How generous of you and Clyde."

"We'll be glad to have you," she said with true southern hospitality.

We packed up the children and moved next door. The Franks were crazy about Toddy and Michael, and they seemed to enjoy us being there. We all managed to survive basic living conditions for the time we stayed with them.

"We have a camp stove, so we can cook and warm up the baby's bottles," Grace said. We had hot meals, basic things like canned chili and soup, and I boiled creek water to make baby formula and sterilize the baby bottles, which was what we had to do in those days. I melted snow over the heat registers in the floor for wash water, and I washed Michael's cloth diapers by hand. There were no disposables then! I brought over food from our refrigerator to cook before it would spoil, and that helped me feel like we were contributing to what turned out to be a real adventure.

We stayed with these wonderful neighbors for three days until the power was finally restored. I rather envied those folks in the coal camp who had coal stoves and fireplaces in their primitive houses; they could stay warm and cook, at least, even if they had no lights. Everyone kept candles and kerosene lanterns in case of the occasional power outages we experienced, so they were able to stay in their homes. The experience almost made me regret our complete dependence on modern conveniences, especially electricity. Almost.

A severe ice storm takes down the power lines for the author's neighborhood, making roads impassable and bringing life to a standstill.

When the power was finally restored, we were glad to go home. However, we discovered that the electric surge, caused when the power lines went down, had fried the insides of our new television set. We had to pay almost as much to have it repaired as we'd paid for the set, but once hooked, we decided we couldn't do without it. It brought welcome news and entertainment from the outside world to our isolated area.

Being stranded by the ice storm turned out to be a sober learning experience. All our modern appliances and conveniences were of no use to us, and we had to rely on others for help. We were glad to discover that we could manage, thanks to help from dear friends, to deal with hard times.

CHAPTER 23

The Frontier Nursing Service

One day when the phone rang our ring—one long and two shorts on the party line—it was my friend Sally with a lovely and unexpected invitation.

"Margie, how would you and Steve like to go to tea with Mary Breckinridge?"

"Really?" I was excited. It would be a real treat to meet Mary Breckinridge. She was a celebrity in Leslie County.

"When? And why did she invite us?"

"Well, she called me to come visit on Sunday afternoon and said I could bring guests. So, I thought the two of you might like to go."

Sally had worked as a secretary for Mrs. Breckinridge and the Frontier Nursing Service before her marriage to Paul, and now her younger sister, Kay, had taken the job and lived on-site. Sally often visited at Wendover, the headquarters of the FNS and home of Mrs. Breckinridge.

"That sounds like a lovely adventure," I said, without even consulting Steve.

"I'll pick you up about three on Sunday," she said.

When Steve got home from work that day, I said, "We're going to tea with Mrs. Breckenridge, honey."

He didn't look particularly thrilled about a tea party, but he agreed to go. He knew what amazing things she had done for the people who lived up in the hills and hollers, and he, too, wanted to meet her.

On Sunday afternoon, the four of us drove over dirt roads and forded a crick or two to arrive at a remote area not too far from Hyden. Mrs. Breckinridge's large, beautiful log house, surrounded by a barn and other outbuildings, dominated the peaceful clearing near a bubbling stream.

We were delighted to meet this impressive grande dame. White-haired, handsome, and regal, she welcomed us with the manners of a true southern lady. Probably in her early seventies at that time, she charmed us with her hospitality, intelligence, and wit. She offered us tea and sherry as well, a special treat we were delighted to share, especially in that area where our staunch fundamentalist friends disapproved of liquor in any form. The delicious little cakes, scones, and sandwiches seemed a lovely vestige of Victorian customs.

While we visited, Mrs. Breckinridge told us the story of one of the most remarkable institutions in Leslie County, the Frontier Nursing Service, which she had founded in the 1925. The FNS provided much-needed medical treatment to the local people who lived up in the isolated hills and hollers of Leslie County, and most especially to pregnant women and new mothers. The nurses were all trained midwives, who rode mules and horses up into the hills where there were no roads in order to deliver babies and teach the mothers how to care for their newborns, and the other children too, using modern antiseptic care.

She hired nurse-midwives from Great Britain at first. They cared for the hill women and babies there and became teachers of midwifery for the other nurses who came later. The nurses also took care of minor health problems for the whole family. Serious problems then meant calling for a doctor to ride horseback the 25 miles over the mountains from Hazard to treat the patient, and sometimes he arrived too late to help. Now serious problems went to the Hyden Hospital, built later by Mrs. Breckinridge, where there was a doctor to treat them.

We were impressed by all that Mary Breckinridge had accomplished for the people of Leslie County. We found it exhilarating to visit with such a widely traveled, well-educated woman who could talk intelligently on many subjects, and we found it hard to tear ourselves away from Wendover.

It wasn't until recently, when I read her book, *Wide Neighborhoods*, that I learned more about this amazing woman. Mary was born into a well-known Kentucky family, the great-granddaughter of John C. Breckinridge, a vice president of the United States, who was exiled to England after the Civil War for his Southern sympathies.

She spent her teenage years in St. Petersburg, Russia, where her father was stationed as a diplomat. She was tutored at home, attended a private boarding school for girls in Switzerland, and a finishing school for girls in Connecticut. This kind of education hardly prepared her for living in the remote hills of Appalachia or building and running a complex medical system, but it was obvious she had learned later what she needed to know to administer her large enterprise.

Mary's first marriage ended when her husband died. Wanting to be of some use to society, she then attended nursing school. She remarried a few years later and had two children. The oldest, a little boy called Breckie, died at age three, and a daughter was stillborn. When that marriage ended unhappily, she assumed her maiden name. The tragic losses of her children led Mary to want to devote her life to others, especially to children.

After World War I, she spent time in France as a nurse, working with children and pregnant women and founding a visiting nurse service there. Deciding that was what was needed back in the U.S., she trained as a mid-wife in England and Scotland to learn the skills she would need here.

When Mary came home from France, she surveyed areas where she wanted to establish her nursing service. She chose Kentucky partly because of ties with Breckinridge relatives, who would help her financially, and partly because of the lack of medical facilities in these isolated counties. Dr. Arthur McCormack, health commissioner for the Commonwealth of Kentucky, who approved the necessary certification to establish her project, suggested that she build her first center " ... in Leslie County, in the heart of a thousand-square-mile area covering parts of several counties, where some fifteen thousand people lived without benefit of one resident state-licensed physician." [3]

Traveling by horseback all over the mountains of Kentucky—there were no roads into the area in the 1920s—she found the care of women in childbirth and their babies to be medieval and knew this was where she wanted to serve. She discovered the site for Wendover on the Middle Fork of the Kentucky River, up Muncy Creek, and decided that's where she would establish her home and the nursing service.

A bubbling creek near Wendover, where Mary Breckinridge
established the Frontier Nursing Service headquarters.

In 1925, she officially opened the Frontier Nursing Service, dedicating it to her two lost children. It was to become a lifetime job for Mary Breckinridge, and she personally financed it for its first three years. Money was always a problem, but Mary had wonderful support from her Kentucky relatives and groups she organized in large cities all

---

[3] Ibid, p. 158

over the East. It seemed that every time she had a desperate need, a gift of money showed up.

Leslie County covers 376 square miles of rough terrain, and the difficulties Mary encountered were often overwhelming. At that time, there were no roads for sixty miles; all the supplies she needed to build her dream had to be brought in through the heavily wooded mountains by horseback or mule and wagon, occasionally even by river rafts. They suffered many difficulties with bad weather, snow and ice, rain and floods, and extreme heat, which made it a terrible struggle to transport all the supplies they needed for their building program.

She erected every building of her facility using local labor and as many local resources as possible, felling native trees for the lumber. They had enormous problems trying to build modern structures with plumbing and electricity in a remote area where the workmen had never even seen such modern conveniences. Just getting electric lines into Wendover through the rough countryside was a formidable job. Fortunately, she was able to bring in a construction foreman from the "outside." One can just imagine how difficult it was to teach his backwoods workmen to become plumbers and electricians when they'd never had plumbing or electricity in their homes.

Mary built her headquarters at Wendover, first a log cabin in 1925, then a barn, then a three-story log house. She started her nursing service in a small two-story building in bad repair, which she fixed up to suit her purposes. She had two nurses at first, and they traveled by horse and mule up into the hills and hollers, along rivers and creeks, and over rough trails. The people of Leslie County were immediately receptive to the traveling nurses. It was a long distance to the nearest medical help, and many people had died before a doctor could arrive after a ten- or twelve-hour horseback trip from Hazard, where the nearest doctors lived and practiced.

Although the local people were for the most part uneducated, Mary found them wonderfully helpful, honest, and hardworking— just as we found when we arrived in Leslie County. Her nurses felt safe traveling alone along the lonely trails of the hill country. She said that the native Kentuckians had retained the "pioneer code of honor" and were chivalrous to women. "Wherever you find a highland people, they are the seed corn of the world," said Judge Edward C. O'Rear, of Frankfort, at the Frontier Nursing Service dedication in 1928.[4]

Later she would expand her outreach with the building of Hyden Hospital and Health Center, a medical director's quarters, the graduate school, a lab, and an x-ray building. By 1952, when she wrote her history of the FNS, Mary still had horses and mules for the nurses' transportation, but she also had twelve World War II army jeeps that could traverse the rough trails up the hollers where there were still no roads. She also had a station wagon ambulance and a truck, which greatly improved her ability to reach people in need of help.

By the time we arrived in Kentucky, the health of the hill people of Leslie County had been much improved—thanks to the foresight and vision of this hardworking, determined, and remarkable woman who dedicated so much of her life to caring for the welfare of her people. She had brought twentieth-century medicine to people that were still living in eighteenth-century conditions.

We still treasure our memories of the lovely time we spent with Mary Breckinridge. We felt privileged to meet this selfless and determined woman who accomplished her dream in spite of so many obstacles. The time we spent with her will always be one of the highlights of our time in Kentucky.

---

[4] Ibid, p. 224

CHAPTER 24

Moving On

"Steve, we need to talk."

We were sitting at the dining room table, having finished dinner and put the boys to bed. It was quiet with them asleep and a good time to bring up a problem I'd been worrying about.

"What's on your mind?"

"I've been thinking about the boys' education." Toddy was almost five and would soon be ready for school.

"I've been thinking about that too, knowing about the little school here."

The coal camp school was primitive: a small one-room building with no running water, an outhouse out back, and a potbellied coal stove to heat it in winter. The impoverished county school district could not pay competitive salaries for certified teachers; they were lucky to find a high school graduate to teach in the isolated county schools. And that teacher had to teach all eight grades at the same time, a challenge for even a trained, experienced teacher.

"Do we really want them to go to school here in the coal camp?"

"Not really," he said. "But what's the alternative?"

"Maybe I could do some homeschooling to supplement what the coal camp school offered, and I even thought about applying for the job as the teacher here," I said, "but I was trained in secondary education and have no skills in teaching little ones to read and write. I probably wouldn't do any better than those teachers who come and go like swinging doors. Besides, I don't want to leave Michael with a babysitter while I go off to work."

"Of course, Margie, but if they don't go to the little school here, where else could they go? If not here, you do know that means we would have to move away from the coal camp."

"I know," I said. "That's the big problem. I love our home and our friends here. And I know how much you love your job here. It's a pretty huge thing to give up everything we have now and venture to a new place."

"Well, we do need to think seriously about it," Steve said. "You're right that the school situation is a big concern."

Toddy looks lovingly at his daddy, Steve Conder. He would soon be ready to go to school.

Education was not a big priority among the mountain people at that time. We had learned that many of the older local people were illiterate, and many of the younger ones had not even finished high school. When Steve drove to the bank in Manchester to pick up the payroll for the coal company, he discovered that all the miners were paid in cash rather than checks. Many did not trust banks, and some of them could not even write their names. He witnessed men signing for their pay with a big X.

One year, I was heartened to learn that the Ford Foundation had subsidized the salary for two trained and certified teachers to teach at one of the schools in a nearby mountain settlement. Unfortunately, they did not finish out the year. It wasn't just the primitive conditions; many of the local folk didn't like the newfangled notions those teachers brought with them.

"What was good enuf for my gran-pappy is good enuf for me" seemed to be the local philosophy, and the people of that community were resistant to new ideas, especially when they came from furriners.

Both of us had been lucky enough to enjoy good educations, and we wanted the same privilege for our children. Reluctantly, we began to think about moving on to a place that would offer them a better chance for that. Neither of us really wanted to leave.

However, we had another reason to think of moving away. The damp weather, especially during the long winter months, aggravated Michael's asthmatic bronchitis. He often had croup, a very scary condition when he coughed so hard that he almost passed out. He just couldn't get his breath—even when we sat with him in a hot, steamy bathroom, trying to ease the tight, harsh coughing. We had to take him to the doctor in Hazard to get an antibiotic so often that I worried about his ability to fight off infections without them.

"Do you think," I asked Steve, "that Michael's bronchitis would benefit from our living in a drier climate? Maybe he wouldn't get sick so often."

"You're right, Margie, but that would mean leaving here," Steve said.

"I know. And I know how much you love your work here in the Kentucky coal mines. I hate that we even have to *consider* leaving."

"Let me think about it for a while, honey. I'm sure I can get work in other mining areas, but we have it pretty good here, don't we? He sighed.

"Of course, we do, and I love our life here, too. I guess I'm looking ahead to next year. It's time for Toddy to go to kindergarten, and there's none here."

"Let me think about it, Margie," he said. "I'm sure it would be better

137

for the boys if we moved, but it would be tough for me to give up my good job."

"I understand, Steve. And if you don't want to go somewhere else, I'll go along with whatever you decide. We can work it out somehow." I wrapped my arms around him, knowing just how difficult a decision it was for him to leave the job he loved. If he really didn't want to move, we would manage.

We did have another concern besides the issues of the boys' schooling and Michael's bronchitis. The recurrence of yearly spring floods on our little crick was getting more serious every year. Each spring, following heavy winter rains, Cutshin Creek became a monster, rising high enough to cover part of Clyde and Grace's yard and tickle at ours. I watched as houses and other buildings roared downstream to smash against the bridge. As much as I loved our home, I didn't relish living in a floodplain, and our house definitely fit the bill. Indeed, the year after we left, both the Franks' home and the house we'd lived in were flooded up to the middle of the windows. We were fortunate to have left before that flood. Everything we owned would have been lost. There is no way to turn off the water faucet in the bathtub of a raging river.

Cutshin Creek floods the former home of the Conders in 1956, the spring after they left Kentucky. Water line shows high water level at middle of the window.

The school situation, Michael's bronchial infections, and the threat of yearly floods did give Steve the impetus to begin looking for jobs back in the West, where he had contacts from Colorado School of Mines. He began to send out resumes, and in the late spring of 1955, he received an attractive offer from the Potash Company of America—in New Mexico.

"Margie," he said as he waved a letter at me. "I got a job offer in Carlsbad."

"Oh, that's wonderful!" I hugged him hard.

"I hate to leave coal mining, but potash mining is similar to working with coal, and it does have a better safety record."

"For that, I am thankful," I said. "Also, the schools will probably be better, and the dry climate will be healthier for Michael. But I know how much you love your job here, and I do appreciate how difficult it will be for you to leave it. I'll also be sad to leave these beautiful mountains and my friends here, too, especially Sally. Change is not fun."

"Even so, I think I should accept the offer," he said ruefully. Though he hated leaving Kentucky and coal mining, he had made up his mind. The job in Carlsbad sounded good, better pay, better schools, better climate. "They want me to come as soon as possible. Can you start packing?"

"Absolutely," I said, not knowing whether to be sad or glad or both.

We prepared to leave our home in the mountains of Kentucky. It would be an expensive move since we had to pay for the cost of the moving van. I got rid of as many heavy items as I could, discarding big college textbooks and other items we really didn't need. I sold the dining room furniture to a neighbor, gave away some non-essential items, did much of the packing myself to cut down on costs. Finally, we were ready for the movers.

We both felt devastated to part with dear friends and those ancient, beautiful mountains of Kentucky. Sally and I wept as we hugged our goodbye, and I had tears in my eyes saying farewell to the McGees and Grace. I had learned so much about life from these good people, and I was grateful for what they had taught me about life, culture, language, respect, and friendship. I had come as a young, inexperienced college graduate who thought I knew everything, and I felt like I was leaving as a more mature young woman who had learned that not all wisdom comes from books and schooling—along with many other valuable life lessons.

We headed to Carlsbad to write a new chapter in our lives. It would be a happy one. There, we would become parents of a beloved daughter, buy a home of our own, and make many new friends. Toddy started school there and thrived. Michael's croup improved, too.

Today, though, I remember those four years in Appalachia as some of the very best times of our lives. Although our experiences were far from what I imagined life in the South would be, I will always remember it as a wonderful and rewarding time.

Even though it was difficult at first for me to be so far from family and friends and my familiar comfort zone, learning to adapt to different ways and making new friends brought me deep satisfaction. I learned a great deal about the joys of southern cooking and homemaking and getting along with people who were different from me.

The challenges we faced helped me become an adult, and I felt far more confident in my ability to handle tough situations than I had been four years earlier. As I matured, I broadened my outlook and was able to better appreciate the differences among people and their cultures. I had grown up.

Our time in Kentucky brought us many other gifts. We had become financially secure after our first two impoverished years of marriage, starting a family while still in college. We now felt rich in our family—with our two little boys—and the home we had established. Most especially, we both gained a better ability to deal with life and change and love and loss. Even though we came as furriners, we left with firm friendships and a feeling of belonging.

Our adventure in Appalachia enriched our lives in so many ways, and we deeply cherish the wonderful memories of our four years in the hills of Kentucky.

The author and her husband, no longer "furriners," felt sad to leave friends and the beautiful mountains of Appalachia. View from the front porch of the Conder home in 1955.